REVISE 11+

Also available to support
English 11+ revision:

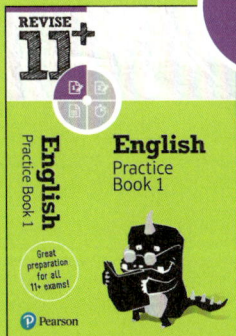

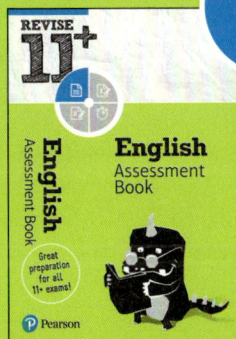

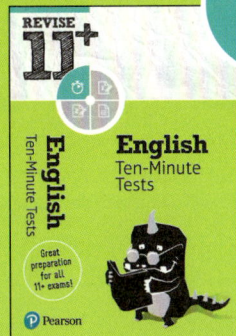

REVISE 11+

English
Practice Book 1

English
Practice
Book 1

Great
preparation
for all
11+ exams!

Pearson

REVISE 11+

English
Assessment Book

English
Assessment
Book

Great
preparation
for all
11+ exams!

Pearson

REVISE 11+

English
Ten-Minute Tests

English
Ten-Minute
Tests

Great
preparation
for all
11+ exams!

Pearson

English
Practice
Book 2

Series Consultant: Harry Smith
Author: Helen Thomson

THE REVISE 11⁺ SERIES

For the full range of Pearson Revise 11⁺ titles visit:
www.pearsonschools.co.uk/revise11plus

Pearson

Contents

How to use this book

Complete the *Diagnostic test*.

Study the *Worked examples*.

Use the hints and support to answer the *Guided questions*.

Your 11+ journey

Diagnostic test

Complete this test before you start any of the practice sections. It covers all the topics in this book and is as hard as a real 11+ test, so don't worry if you get a lot of answers wrong. It will help you see which topics you need to practise the most.

Comprehension (30)

This non-fiction text is from a newspaper article.

How to find a missing pet

Every year hundreds of family pets go missing from their homes. This is very upsetting for their owners, who go to considerable lengths to trace their beloved animals and often offer hefty rewards for their safe return.

Unsurprisingly, dogs and cats are the most likely pets to go missing. Dogs commonly break from their leads or get lost on walks, while cats are often at risk after a house move. This is because cats are territorial and, if they get out before they have established themselves in their new territory, will try to make their way back to their old home.

If your pet goes missing you should stay calm and follow these practical steps:
- organise a search party in the locality
- check any sheds and garages and ask your neighbours to do the same
- put up posters in the local area with a photograph of your pet and your contact number
- contact your local police station and veterinary surgeons
- contact your local newspaper.

If you are still unable to locate your pet, don't give up hope. There have been cases of animals (even tortoises) turning up at their owner's home after many years.

1 Which type of text is this? Tick *one* box. **Section 10**
☐ story ☐ instructional text ☐ biography ☐ historical account

2 What feature does the writer use to present the instructions for owners with missing pets? Write your answer below. **Section 10**

...own ambition... these words details to a sentence but out by a pair of commas, brackets or dashes.

Worked examples

1 Which sentence below uses parenthesis? Tick *one* box.
☐ The new sports centre includes a huge pool and
☑ Wombats (like all marsupials) rear their young in
☐ Belgian chocolate is famous throughout the wor
☐ I can't run because the soles of my feet are achin

2 Underline the parenthesis in the sentence below.
Hayley, <u>whose sister is a friend of yours</u>, is havin

3 Rewrite the sentence below, adding dashes to punctua
Aunt Julie arrived with presents which was com and little Zoey screamed in delight.

Guided questions

1 Which sentence below uses a parenthesis? Tick *one* box.
☐ Look – the procession is parading through the tow
☐ You can find examples of Roman ruins throughout
☐ We were feeling – as you can imagine – quite nervo
☐ Imani's ambition has always been to become a den high salary.

2 Underline the parenthesis in the sentence below.
Abraham Lincoln (a famous American president) w

3 Rewrite the sentence below using dashes to punctuate th
Finlay running around hopelessly as usual couldn'
Finlay - running

Work independently in the *Have a go* section. The orange difficulty dials will tell you how challenging each question is.

Complete the *Timed practice* in test conditions.

Take a break with *Beyond the exam* activities.

Timed practice

1 Which sentence below uses a parenthesis? Tick *one*
☐ Lerwick, which is the only town in the Shetland
☐ My Grandmother will be 95 next month and is
☐ We will play hockey on Saturday if the pitch is
☐ I can't wait until Saturday – we are getting a n

2 Underline the parenthesis in the sentence below.
Last time we spoke – which was just before Ch

3 Rewrite the sentence below using brackets or comm
Elephants which are the largest mammals on

Have a go

1 Which sentence below uses a parenthesis? Tick *one*
☐ Beat cream cheese, sugar and vanilla with a mi
☐ Look at that field – it's full of beautiful sunflow
☐ My local shopping centre has a wide variety of sportswear shops, boutiques, bookshops and f
☐ The Yangtze River, which is 6380 km long, is the

[1 mark]

2 Underline the parenthesis in the sentence below.
Horticulture (the art of growing plants) is beco

[1 mark]

3 Rewrite the sentence below using commas to punctu
My eldest brother who is five years older than

[1]

6 Is the statement below true or false? Tick *one* b
'Because of' is a prepositional phrase of ca
☑ true ☐ false

Beyond the exam

Well-known sayings, like the one in question 5, are idioms. Find out what the three idioms below mean haven't heard before.
- A bird in the hand is worth two in the bush.
- Birds of a feather flock together.
- Barking up the wrong tree.

Track your progress on the *Progress chart* and follow the instructions in the *Time to reflect* box.

Practise mixed questions in the *Checkpoints*.

Complete your revision with the *Progress test*.

6 In which section is the mistake in the sentence below?
In my pencil case / there is a / pencil a rubber a
1   2   3

Time to reflect

Mark your Timed practice   section out of 9. H
Check your answers in the back of the book and write your s

☐ **0–7 marks**
Scan the QR code for extra practice.
Then move on to the next practice section or try Test 3 in your Ten-Minute Tests book.

Checkpoint 1

In this checkpoint you will practise skills from the **Grammar and punctuation** topic.

1 Punctuate the parenthesis in this sentence using dashes. (15)
If our team wins the match on Saturday and everyone thinks they will we will all go and watch the final next month. **Section 1**

2 Which sentence is punctuated correctly? Tick *one* box.
☐ The firemen's helmets are designed to protect them from heat and falling cinders. **Section 6**
☐ The firemen's helmets are designed to protect them from heat and falling cinders.
☐ The firemen's helmets are designed to protect them from heat and falling cinders.

3 Rewrite the following sentence using the correct punctuation. **Section 4**
My favourite films are action movies said Joshua

4 Which preposition of place completes the sentence below? Tick *one* box. **Section 2**
The post office is situated _____ the newsagents and the launderette.
☐ between ☐ on ☐ in ☐ at

5 Which sentence is punctuated correctly? Tick *one* box. **Section 5**

Progress test

Complete this test once you have worked through all the practice sections. It covers all the topics in this book and is as hard as a real 11+ test.

Comprehension (50)

Tropical Rainforests

Tropical rainforests are dense areas of jungle covering approximately 7 per cent of the Earth's surface. The main areas of tropical rainforest are located in South and Central America, West Africa and Indonesia. All these areas are situated around the Equator and have very warm and wet climates. The high precipitation (some rainforests can receive up to 300 mm of rain per month), combined with average temperatures of around 28°C, provides ideal conditions for an abundance of animals, insects and plants to thrive. Rainforests also produce 20 per cent of the world's oxygen, which is vital for our survival.

The largest tropical rainforest in the world is Amazonia in South America. This vast area of dense jungle is criss-crossed by thousands of rivers and their tributaries, including the second longest river in the world – the Amazon. Amazonia covers an enormous area that could swallow Great Britain around 26 times over. It includes most of north-western Brazil and spans six other countries. Amazonia has extraordinary biodiversity and it is estimated that it is home to 2.5 million species of insects, 1500 types of birds, over 2000 fish species and 4000 varieties of plants.

Tropical rainforests are often referred to as the world's largest pharmacy. This is because a quarter of all natural medicines have been discovered in the plants that grow there, and there may still be many more for scientists to find. In addition to medicines, rubber, chocolate, bamboo, nuts and vanilla are all produced by rainforest plants.

In light of all these benefits, you would think that mankind would fiercely protect the rainforests. Sadly, though, this is not the case. Rainforests are rapidly shrinking as large areas are cut down to clear space for logging, farming, mining and building.

So why is this destruction permitted? The governments of many poorer countries feel that they have no choice, as the resources and land in the rainforest are an importance source of income and jobs for ever-growing populations. In order to protect what is left of the rainforest, we must find a way to support and develop these countries so that they can use their resources in a more sustainable way. A balance must be found between the needs of nature and the needs of humankind.

1 Find and copy a word that means 'the variety of animal and plant life in an area'. **Section 10**
_____

Move on to the Ten-Minute Tests and Assessment Workbook ◀

Diagnostic test

Complete this test before you start any of the practice sections. It covers all the topics in this book and is as hard as a real 11+ test, so don't worry if you get a lot of answers wrong. It will help you see which topics you need to practise the most.

Comprehension

60

This non-fiction text is from a newspaper article.

How to find a missing pet

Every year hundreds of family pets go missing from their homes. This is very upsetting for their owners, who go to considerable lengths to trace their beloved animals and often offer hefty rewards for their safe return.

Unsurprisingly, dogs and cats are the most likely pets to go missing. Dogs commonly break from their leads or get lost on walks, while cats are often at risk after a house move. This is because cats are territorial and, if they get out before they have established themselves in their new territory, will try to make their way back to their old home.

If your pet goes missing you should stay calm and follow these practical steps:
- organise a search party in the locality
- check any sheds and garages and ask your neighbours to do the same
- put up posters in the local area with a photograph of your pet and your contact number
- contact your local police station and veterinary surgeons
- contact your local newspaper.

If you are still unable to locate your pet, don't give up hope. There have been cases of animals (even tortoises) turning up at their owner's home after many years.

1 mark

1 Which type of text is this? Tick **one** box.

→ Section 10

☐ story ☐ instructional text ☐ biography ☐ historical account

1 mark

2 What feature does the writer use to present the instructions for owners with missing pets? Write your answer below.

→ Section 10

_____

1 mark

3 Find and copy a word that means 'attached to a particular area'.

→ Section 10

_____

1 mark

4 Find and copy a phrase that means 'settled in'.

→ Section 10

_____

1 mark

5 Why is the last paragraph an effective ending to the text? Tick **one** box.

→ Section 11

☐ It gives instructions about what do if a pet is lost.

☐ It provides an introduction to the text.

☐ It gives the reader hope.

☐ It sends out an appeal to find a lost pet.

This is from a short story called 'Kew Gardens' by Virginia Woolf. In this section, two women are walking through the park.

Following his steps so closely as to be slightly puzzled by his gestures came two elderly women of the lower middle class, one stout and ponderous, the other rosy cheeked and nimble.

"Nell, Bert, Lot, Cess, Phil, Pa, he says, she says, I says, I says – "

The ponderous woman looked through the pattern of falling words at the flowers standing cool, firm and upright in the earth, with a curious expression. She saw them as a sleeper waking from a heavy sleep sees a brass candlestick reflecting the light in an unfamiliar way, and closes his eyes and opens them, and seeing the brass candlestick again, finally starts broad awake and stares at the candlestick with all his powers. So the heavy woman came to a standstill opposite the oval-shaped flower bed, and ceased even to pretend to listen to what the other woman was saying. She stood there letting the words fall over her, swaying the top part of her body slowly backwards and forwards, looking at the flowers. Then she suggested that they should find a seat and have tea.

abc 'Ponderous' means 'slow and clumsy'

6 Why is the second paragraph in speech marks? Write your answer below.

← Section 10

1 mark

_____

7 Find and copy a word that means 'light and quick'.

← Section 10

1 mark

_____

8 a The nimble woman's speech is described as a 'pattern of falling words'. What literary device is this? Write your answer below.

← Section 10

_____

b How does the ponderous woman feel about what the nimble woman is saying? Tick **one** box.

← Section 11

☐ She is not very interested in what the nimble woman is saying.

☐ She is bored with talking about the rain.

☐ The nimble woman's words sound like rain to her because she isn't listening properly.

☐ She is annoyed because the nimble woman is saying something mean.

2 marks

9 a Is the ponderous woman really listening to what the nimble woman is saying? Write your answer below.

← Section 11

_____

b What phrase tells you this? Find and copy it.

_____

2 marks

10 Is the ponderous woman wrong to not pay attention to her friend? Explain your opinion.

← Section 12

_____
_____
_____

1 mark

This fiction extract is from 'Stolen Destinies' by Helen M Thomson. It is set in Oman many years ago. In this section, a girl is travelling through the mountains.

Miriam pulled aside the tent flap and stared up at the twisted folds of rocky mountainside. She scanned the barren slopes in the small hope of a reminder of home – a palm tree or tended field – but not even a shrivelled bush survived amongst the ruptured layers of limestone and shale. Bare rock face rose up above her, a petrified tidal wave poised to engulf the encampment. If only there was some sign of life. If only there was some gentle, green patch however small, a promise of tenderness to soften the blistering rocks and razor peaks, but there was none. Fear bore down on her like molten lava.

She wandered to the campfire and crouched beside the flames, palms outstretched. The encampment hummed with activity. The chink of pestle and mortar rang out as the servants ground the coffee. She watched as her tent was collapsed and her belongings bundled up. Then, after much to-ing, fro-ing and shouting of instructions and conflicting instructions, during which camels were loaded, unloaded and reloaded, the caravan set off again.

abc
- An encampment is a group of tents.
- A caravan is a large group of people travelling together.

11 a What do you think Miriam feels when she looks out at the mountains? Write your answer below.

← Section 10

_____

_____

_____

b Which phrase tells you this? Find and copy it.

| 2 |
| marks |

_____

12 What does the word 'petrified' mean in this text? Tick **one** box.

← Section 10

☐ terrified

☐ transformed into stone

☐ dry and dusty

☐ enormous

| 1 |
| mark |

| 1 |
| mark |

13 Find and copy a word that means 'bare and without vegetation'.

← Section 10

_____

14 The mountains are described as 'razor peaks'. What does this tell you about them? Write your answer below.

← Section 11

| 1 |
| mark |

_____

_____

| 1 |
| mark |

15 Find and copy an example of onomatopoeia.

← Section 10

_____

This is an extract from the poem 'Dulce et decorum est' by Wilfred Owen. It is about soldiers leaving the battlefield during the First World War.

Dulce et decorum est

Bent double, like old beggars under sacks,

Knock-kneed, coughing like hags, we cursed through sludge,

Till on the haunting flare we turned our backs,

And towards our distant rest began to trudge.

Men marched asleep. Many had lost their boots,

But limped on, blood-shod. All went lame; all blind;

Drunk with fatigue; deaf even to the hoots

Of tired, outstripped Five-Nines that dropped behind.

abc
- The title 'Dulce et decorum est' comes from a Latin phrase that means 'it is sweet and honourable to die for your country'.
- Five-Nines are rockets containing poison gas.

16 a What does the poet compare the soldiers to in the first line? Write your answer below.

Section 13

_____

b Which literary device is this? Write your answer below.

_____

2 marks

17 The soldiers were 'drunk with fatigue'. What does this mean? Tick **one** box.

Section 13

☐ The soldiers had been drinking alcohol.　　☐ The soldiers were so tired they felt drunk.

☐ The soldiers didn't feel tired at all.　　☐ The soldiers couldn't hear anything.

1 mark

18 Explain what the phrase 'blood-shod' tells you.

Section 13

_____

1 mark

19 a Find and copy one example of alliteration.

Section 13

_____

b What does this tell you about the way the soldiers are moving?

_____

_____

2 marks

20 Do you think the poet believes that it is 'sweet and honourable to die for your country'? Give reasons for your opinion.

Section 13

_____

_____

_____

_____

2 marks

Spelling, punctuation and grammar

21 Which sentence below uses parenthesis correctly? Tick **one** box.

Section 1

☐ Thunder storms, can be very beautiful to watch, but can cause huge damage.

☐ Thunder storms can cause huge damage and are very beautiful to watch.

☐ Thunder storms, although often very beautiful to watch, can cause huge damage.

☐ (Thunder storms) can be very beautiful to watch and can cause huge damage.

1 mark

22 Punctate the sentence below using a colon.

Section 5

John F. Kennedy said 'Those who dare to fail miserably can achieve greatly.'

1 mark

23 Rewrite the sentence below using a possessive apostrophe.

Section 6

The changing room belonging to the ladies is on the left.

1 mark

24 Circle the correct spelling to complete the sentence below.

Section 8

Before the visit we were given a (brief / brief) talk about the area.

1 mark

25 Which sentence below is punctuated correctly? Tick **one** box.

Section 6

☐ An alligators' bite will almost always prove fatal.   ☐ An alligato'rs bite will almost always prove fatal.

☐ An alligator's bite will almost always prove fatal.   ☐ An alligators bite will almost always prove fatal.

1 mark

26 Underline the correct homophone in brackets in the sentence below.

Section 7

The soldier won a (medal / meddle) for her bravery.

1 mark

27 Write a sentence using a preposition of time describing when you do your homework.

Section 2

1 mark

28 Underline the prepositional phrase in the sentence below.

Section 2

The audience was held spellbound throughout the performance.

1 mark

29 Write a sentence about a sport, using a coordinating conjunction.

Section 3

1 mark

30 a Underline the preposition in the sentence below. Section 2

The train was hurtling towards the station.

b What type of preposition is this? Tick **one** box.

☐ time

☐ place

☐ direction

☐ cause

2 marks

31 Is the statement below true or false? Tick **one** box. Section 1

If you remove the parenthesis from a sentence, it still makes sense.

☐ true   ☐ false

1 mark

32 Circle the correct homophone in brackets in the sentence below. Section 7

Grandma puts orange (peal / peel) in Christmas cake for extra flavour.

1 mark

33 Punctuate the sentence below using semi-colons. Section 5

To stay safe online you should never do these things: communicate with anyone you do not know send photos, personal information or details about where you live send messages to anyone without your parents' or guardians' permission or arrange to meet anyone you have met online.

1 mark

34 Rewrite the sentence below punctuating the parenthesis correctly. Section 1

The community centre which is where the pottery classes take place also has an art gallery.

_____

_____

1 mark

35 Complete the sentence below with a list of items you need to take to school. Section 5

You will need to take _____

_____

1 mark

36 Underline the preposition of time in the sentence below. Section 2

The new school term starts on Tuesday 3 September.

1 mark

37 a Underline the conjunction in the sentence below. Section 3

It is very cold today but it is sunny.

b Which type of conjunction this? Tick **one** box.

☐ subordinating   ☐ coordinating

2 marks

38 Rewrite the sentence below using the correct punctuation.

Section 4

blue is my favourite colour said Arthur

1 mark

39 Complete the sentence below using the correct conjunction.

Section 3

Dad always takes us to the funfair _____ we visit the seaside.

1 mark

although   whenever   because   why

40 Which sentence below is correctly punctuated? Tick **one** box.

Section 6

☐ The ancient oak tree lay on the ground, its trunk split in half.

☐ The ancient oak tree lay on the ground, it's trunk split in half.

☐ The ancient oak tree lay on the ground, its' trunk split in half.

☐ The ancient oak tree lay on the ground, its's trunk split in half.

1 mark

41 Tick the word that with an **ough** sound that rhymes with 'off'.

Section 8

☐ though

☐ cough

☐ brought

1 mark

42 The text below has the correct punctuation but incorrect layout. Mark the places where a new paragraph should begin using double slashes (//).

Section 4

'How long have you been collecting autographs?' asked Ethan. 'For three years now,' Kwame replied, 'I have thirty three famous people's signatures.' 'Wow! That's a lot!' exclaimed Ethan, who was clearly impressed, 'Who is the most famous person you have an autograph from?'

1 mark

43 Is the statement below true or false? Tick **one** box.

Section 2

'At' can be either a preposition of time or place.

☐ true

☐ false

1 mark

44 In which section is the mistake in the sentence below? Circle the correct number.

Section 4

'Do you know / where dates / come from? asked / Patricia for the third time that day.

1 mark

1   2   3   4

45 Rewrite the sentence below using a contraction.

    I have not seen that film yet.

Section 6

`1` mark

46 Underline the parenthesis in the sentence below.

    Nikkita, who is a dental assistant, works in the centre of town.

Section 1

`1` mark

47 Punctuate the sentence below using a possessive apostrophe.

    It is the British peoples right to vote for the Prime Minister of their choice.

Section 6

`1` mark

48 In which section is the mistake in the sentence below? Circle the correct number.

    I'll collect all the / leaflets and once theyv'e / been divided into piles / we'll deliver them.

        1   2   3   4

Section 6

`1` mark

49 Is the statement below true or false? Tick **one** box.

    You don't need to add an **s** when adding a possessive apostrophe to a plural noun.

    ☐ true

    ☐ false

Section 6

`1` mark

Time to reflect

Mark your *Diagnostic test* out of 57. How did you do?

☐ *0–46 marks*
Start your 11+ preparation by beginning at practice section 1 and working through the whole book.

☐ *47–57 marks*
Use the section links to identify your strengths and weaknesses. You could start by looking at the practice sections you scored the lowest in.

1 Parenthesis

Extra information that adds detail to a sentence but is not essential to its meaning is called a **parenthesis**. It is marked out by a pair of commas, brackets or dashes.

Worked examples

1 Which sentence below uses parenthesis? Tick **one** box.

☐ The new sports centre includes a huge pool and table tennis courts.

☑ Wombats (like all marsupials) rear their young in a pouch.

☐ Belgian chocolate is famous throughout the world.

☐ I can't run because the soles of my feet are aching.

abc There are three different ways of punctuating the parenthesis: brackets, commas and dashes.

The text in brackets is the parenthesis in this sentence. If you remove the parenthesis, the sentence still makes sense.

2 Underline the parenthesis in the sentence below.

Hayley, whose sister is a friend of yours, is having a party on Saturday.

abc A marsupial is a type of mammal that carries its young in a pouch.

3 Rewrite the sentence below, adding dashes to punctuate the parenthesis.

Aunt Julie arrived with presents which was completely unexpected and little Zoey screamed in delight.

Aunt Juliet arrived with presents – which was completely
unexpected – and little Zoey screamed in delight.

The parenthesis here is a **relative clause**. It adds extra information about the subject of the sentence.

4 Rewrite the sentence below, adding the parenthesis 'developed from frogspawn' in brackets.

The tadpoles turn into frogs within 24 hours.

The tadpoles (developed from frogspawn) turn into frogs within 24 hours.

Try reading the sentence with different parts left out. The part you can leave out without affecting the sense of the sentence is the parenthesis.

5 Rewrite the sentence below, punctuating the parenthesis.

Jess closely followed by her best friend William was the first person to swim across the river.

Jess, closely followed by her best friend William, was the first person
to swim across the river.

This answer uses commas, but dashes or brackets would also be correct because the question does not specify which type of punctuation to use.

6 In which section is the mistake in the sentence below?
Circle the correct number.

I want to decorate / my – bedroom I'm bored / with the colour – / but Mum won't let me.

1   ②   3   4

The opening dash is in the wrong position. It should come directly after 'bedroom' and before 'I'm' as 'I'm bored with the colour' is the the extra information.

Guided questions

1 Which sentence below uses a parenthesis? Tick **one** box.

> **abc** Brackets, dashes and commas are always used in pairs to punctuate a parenthesis in the middle of a sentence.

☐ Look – the procession is parading through the town centre!

☐ You can find examples of Roman ruins throughout the city.

☐ We were feeling – as you can imagine – quite nervous by this time.

☐ Imani's ambition has always been to become a dentist and earn a high salary.

2 Underline the parenthesis in the sentence below.

> Look for the extra information in the sentence.

Abraham Lincoln (a famous American president) was assassinated in 1865.

3 Rewrite the sentence below using dashes to punctuate the parenthesis.

> Identify the main clause first. It will be the part that makes sense on its own.

Finlay running around hopelessly as usual couldn't find his PE kit.

Finlay - running _____

_____

_____

4 Complete the sentence below by adding a parenthesis explaining that bottlenose dolphins live in warm seas all over the world.

Bottlenose dolphins (which _____

_____ eat fish and squid.

5 Rewrite the sentence below, punctuating the parenthesis.

> Commas are usually used to punctuate relative clauses.

The headteacher of River View High who used to teach at my old school lives quite near to us.

_____

_____

_____

6 Use the words below to write a sentence that includes a parenthesis in brackets.

> There are **two** different pieces of information about Tasha here. Use one for the main sentence and the other for the parenthesis.

my big sister   loves football   Tasha

_____

_____

_____

Have a go

1 Which sentence below uses a parenthesis? Tick **one** box.

> Look for pairs of punctuation around additional information.

☐ Beat cream cheese, sugar and vanilla with a mixer until blended.

☐ Look at that field – it's full of beautiful sunflowers!

☐ My local shopping centre has a wide variety of outlets, including sportswear shops, boutiques, bookshops and fast-food restaurants.

☐ The Yangtze River, which is 6380 km long, is the third longest river in the world.

1 mark

2 Underline the parenthesis in the sentence below.

Horticulture (the art of growing plants) is becoming a popular career choice for many young people.

1 mark

3 Rewrite the sentence below using commas to punctuate the parenthesis.

My eldest brother who is five years older than me goes to secondary school.

_____

_____

1 mark

4 Complete the sentence below by adding and correctly punctuating the parenthesis 'my home town'.

London _____ has a population of 8.788 million people.

1 mark

5 In which section is the punctuation mistake in the sentence below? Circle the correct number.

The shortest day of / the year or the / winter solstice) is / in late December.

1   2   3   4

1 mark

6 Use the words below to write a sentence that includes a parenthesis.

blue whale   weighs up to 200 tons   largest creature on earth

_____

_____

1 mark

Beyond the exam

Find an article in a newspaper or magazine. Highlight all the examples of parenthesis you can find.

Time to reflect

Mark your *Have a go* section out of 6. How are you doing so far?

Check your answers in the back of the book and see how you are doing.

☐ **Had a go**
0–2 marks

☐ **Nearly there**
3–5 marks

☐ **Nailed it!**
6 marks

Have another look at the *Worked examples* on page 10. Then try these questions again.

Look at your incorrect answers. Make sure you understand how to get the correct answer.

Congratulations! Now see whether you can get full marks on the *Timed practice*.

When you are ready, try the *Timed practice* on the next page.

Timed practice ⏱ 15

1 Which sentence below uses a parenthesis? Tick **one** box.

☐ Lerwick, which is the only town in the Shetland Isles, has a population of around 7000 people.

☐ My Grandmother will be 95 next month and is celebrating with a party.

☐ We will play hockey on Saturday if the pitch is repaired.

☐ I can't wait until Saturday – we are getting a new puppy!

1 mark

2 Underline the parenthesis in the sentence below.

Last time we spoke – which was just before Christmas – I told you what happened at school.

1 mark

3 Rewrite the sentence below using brackets or commas to punctuate the parenthesis.

Elephants which are the largest mammals on land suffer because poachers hunt them for their tusks.

_____

_____

_____

1 mark

4 Complete the sentence below by adding a parenthesis that tells you the theme park is called Wonder World. Use dashes to punctuate it.

Unfortunately, our nearest theme park _____ is closed for the winter months.

1 mark

5 Write a sentence that uses a parenthesis to describe something that happened to you at the weekend.

_____

1 mark

6 In which section is the punctuation mistake in the sentence below? Circle the correct number.

Sunbeams, dancing / with dust / particles streamed / through the windows.

1   2   3   4

1 mark

7 Use the words below to write a sentence that includes parenthesis. You can use additional words.

Beijing   capital of China   modern architecture and historic sites

_____

_____

_____

1 mark

Time to reflect

Mark your *Timed practice* section out of 7. How did you do?

Check your answers in the back of the book and write your score in the progress chart.

☐ *0–5 marks*
Scan the QR code for extra practice. Then move on to the next practice section or try Test 5 in your Ten-Minute Tests book.

☐ *6–7 marks*
Well done! Move on to the next practice section or try Test 5 in your Ten-Minute Tests book.

2 Prepositions

Prepositions give information about time, place, direction or cause.

Worked examples

1 Underline the preposition of time in the sentence below.

Rashid arrived at the cinema <u>at</u> six o'clock.

abc A preposition of time describes when something happens.

The preposition 'at' appears twice in this sentence. However, it is used a preposition of place in the phrase 'at the cinema'.

2 a Which preposition completes the sentence below? Tick **one** box.

The lorry drove slowly _____ the roundabout.

☐ between ☐ below ☑ around ☐ beneath

Read the sentence aloud with the different options and consider which one makes the most sense.

b Which type of preposition is it? Tick **one** box.

☐ time ☐ place ☑ direction ☐ cause

abc A preposition of direction describes where or in which direction something is moving.

3 Complete the sentence below using a preposition of place.

Justin's plate is _____on_____ the table.

abc A preposition of place describes where something is or where something happens.

4 Write a sentence about what time you go to bed. Use a preposition of time.

I go to bed after my shower.

'After' is a preposition of time because it shows when the writer goes to bed.

5 Choose the correct preposition to complete the well-known phrase below.

To kill two birds _____with_____ one stone.

from   between   during   with

This means to complete two tasks at once.

abc A prepositional phrase is a group of two or more words that act like a preposition.

6 Is the statement below true or false? Tick **one** box.

'Because of' is a prepositional phrase of cause.

☑ true ☐ false

abc A preposition of cause describes relationships of cause and effect. They help to explain why something has happened.

For example, in the sentence 'Jude was really tired because of all the noise last night', the prepositional phrase 'because of' explains why Jude was tired.

Beyond the exam

Well-known sayings, like the one in question 5, are called **idioms**. In your exam, you may need to know some common idioms. Find out what the three idioms below mean and then look up the meanings of three new ones that you haven't heard before.

- A bird in the hand is worth two in the bush.
- Birds of a feather flock together.
- Barking up the wrong tree.

Guided questions

1 Underline the preposition of direction in the sentence below.

The runners were racing towards the finish line.

> Look for the word that shows what direction the runners are moving in.

2 Which preposition of time completes the sentence below? Tick **one** box.

The musicians are playing _____ Friday evening.

> Read the sentence aloud and see which preposition makes sense.

☐ in   ☐ past   ☐ on   ☐ at

3 Complete the sentence below using a preposition of direction.

The biscuits are in the highest cupboard _____ the kettle.

> The word 'highest' helps you work out which preposition to use.

4 Write a sentence about where you keep your clothes, using a preposition of place.

I keep my clothes _____

5 Choose the correct preposition to complete the well-known phrase below.

It's no use crying _____ spilt milk.

> If you don't know this phrase, look up it to make sure that you choose the correct preposition.

into   down   towards   over

6 Complete the sentence below using a preposition of cause.

School was cancelled today _____ the snow.

> The preposition you choose should help to explain why the school was closed.

7 a Underline the preposition in the sentence below.

Dinosaurs became extinct 65 million years ago.

> Think carefully about the types of preposition listed in part **b**.

b Which type of preposition is it? Tick **one** box.

☐ time   ☐ place   ☐ direction   ☐ cause

Beyond the exam

With a partner, each draw a room that contains a table, chair, cupboard, shelf and door.

1 Sit back to back and each draw five objects in your room. Don't show your partner.

2 Describe the objects in your room to your partner. As you describe your room they should add your objects to their picture. For example, a black and white cat under the chair.

3 Get them to do the same while you draw their objects.

4 When you've both finished describing your rooms, reveal your drawings. They should be identical!

Have a go

1 Underline the preposition of direction in the sentence below.

> The trains travel along the viaduct.

1 mark

> **abc** A viaduct is a bridge that carries a road or railway line over a valley.

2 a Which preposition completes the sentence below? Tick **one** box.

> The car sped _____ the finish line.

☐ during   ☐ between   ☐ towards   ☐ throughout

2 marks

    b Which type of preposition is it? Tick **one** box.

☐ time   ☐ place   ☐ direction   ☐ cause

3 Complete the sentence below using a preposition of time.

> Nobody has lived in that house _____ Christmas.

1 mark

4 Write a sentence about a bicycle, using a preposition of cause.

> _____
>
> _____

1 mark

5 Circle the correct preposition to complete the well-known phrase below.

> Don't make a mountain _____ a molehill.

in front of   next to   out of   along

1 mark

> When you are practising, look up any phrases that you are not familiar with.

6 Is the statement below true or false? Tick **one** box.

> The word 'on' can be both a preposition of time and a preposition of place.

☐ true   ☐ false

1 mark

> Think of a sentence where 'on' is used as a preposition of time and a sentence where it is used as a preposition of place. Consider whether both make sense.

Time to reflect

Mark your *Have a go* section out of 7. How are you doing so far?

Check your answers in the back of the book and see how you are doing.

☐ **Had a go** *0–3 marks*	☐ **Nearly there** *4–6 marks*	☐ **Nailed it!** *7 marks*
Have another look at the *Worked examples* on page 14. Then try these questions again.	Look at your incorrect answers. Make sure you understand how to get the correct answer.	Congratulations! Now see whether you can get full marks on the *Timed practice*.

When you are ready, try the *Timed practice* on the next page.

Timed practice

⏱ **15**

1 Underline the preposition of cause in the sentence below.

We raised forty pounds for charity by having a cake sale.

> 1 mark

2 **a** Which preposition completes the sentence below? Tick **one** box.

We sheltered _____ Tom's huge umbrella.

☐ under   ☐ away from   ☐ at   ☐ on

b Which type of preposition is it? Tick **one** box.

☐ time   ☐ place   ☐ direction   ☐ cause

> 2 marks

3 Complete the sentence below using a preposition of time.

The clock struck loudly _____ midnight.

> 1 mark

4 Write a sentence about your school timetable using a preposition of time.

_____

_____

> 1 mark

5 Circle the correct preposition to complete the well-known phrase below.

The grass is always greener _____ the other side

on   along   under   besides

> 1 mark

6 Is the statement below true or false? Tick **one** box.

The word 'through' is a preposition of time.

☐ true   ☐ false

> 1 mark

Time to reflect

Mark your *Timed practice* section out of 7. How did you do?

Check your answers in the back of the book and write your score in the progress chart.

☐ *0–5 marks*
Scan the QR code for extra practice.
Then move on to the next practice section or try Test 6 in your Ten-Minute Tests book.

☐ *6–7 marks*
Well done!
Move on to the next practice section or try Test 6 in your Ten-Minute Tests book.

3 Conjunctions

Conjunctions link words, phrases or clauses together in a sentence. Use a coordinating conjunction to link two main clauses, two phrases or two words. Use a subordinating conjunction to link a main clause to a subordinate clause.

Worked examples

1 a Underline the conjunction in the sentence below.

The waiter gives us extra ice cream <u>whenever</u> we eat at the restaurant.

b Which type of conjunction is it? Tick **one** box.

☑ subordinating

☐ coordinating

2 Which coordinating conjunction completes the sentence below? Tick **one** box.

Suki loves peanuts, _____ Leo is allergic to them.

☐ nor

☐ or

☐ for

☑ but

abc A clause is a part of a sentence that includes a subject that is actively doing something. Go to practice section 4 in Practice Book 1 to revise sentences and clauses.

abc Subordinating conjunctions link a main clause and a subordinate clause in a sentence.

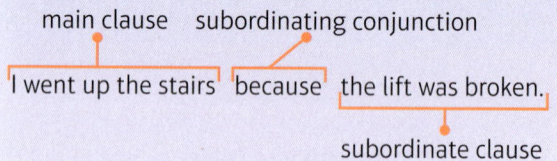

main clause   subordinating conjunction

I went up the stairs   because   the lift was broken.

subordinate clause

abc Coordinating conjunctions link two main clauses in a sentence.

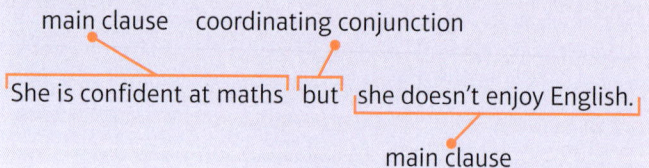

main clause   coordinating conjunction

She is confident at maths   but   she doesn't enjoy English.

main clause

3 Complete the sentence below using the correct subordinating conjunction.

The school stayed open <u>although</u> the central heating had broken down.

why   although   whose   if

4 Complete the sentence below using a coordinating conjunction.

Would you like orange juice <u>or would you prefer lemonade</u> ?

5 Which sentence below uses a subordinating conjunction? Tick **one** box.

☐ They love going to Switzerland, yet they don't like walking in the mountains.

☑ I have to finish my homework before I go out.

abc Subordinating conjunctions can tell you:

- where something happens ('wherever')
- when something happens ('as soon as')
- why something happens ('because').

The clauses in this sentence are of equal importance, so they need a coordinating conjunction.

In this sentence, 'yet' has the same meaning as 'but'. It is a coordinating conjunction.

'I have to finish my homework' is a main clause and 'I go out' is a subordinate clause. 'Before' is a subordinating conjunction.

Guided questions

1 a Underline the conjunction in the sentence below.

Archie loves swimming and Chloe loves paddling.

b Which type of conjunction is it? Tick **one** box.

> Think about whether the two clauses are of equal importance in the sentence.

☐ subordinating

☐ coordinating

2 a Which conjunction completes the sentence below? Tick **one** box.

They waited _____ the rain stopped.

> In this sentence there is a main clause and a subordinate clause.

☐ because

☐ until

☐ or

☐ although

b Which type of conjunction is it?

_____

3 Complete the sentence below using the correct conjunction.

Ashish and Meera were very tired _____ they went to bed early.

why   so   nor   for

4 Which sentence contains a subordinating conjunction? Tick **one** box.

> **abc** Subordinating conjunctions tell us where, when or why something happens.

☐ That is the reason why he wants to leave.

☐ It was raining in the morning, but it was sunny in the afternoon.

5 Is the statement below true or false? Tick **one** box.

Subordinating conjunctions link main clauses in a sentence.

> Think about a sentence that uses a subordinating conjunction, for example 'We will board the train **when** it arrives.'

☐ true

☐ false

Beyond the exam

Choose a newspaper or magazine article. Underline all the conjunctions you can find. Then, highlight the coordinating conjunctions in yellow and the subordinating conjunctions in blue.

Have a go

1 a Underline the conjunction in the sentence below.

Brad wants to get home quickly because his favourite show is on television.

b Which type of conjunction is it? Tick **one** box.

☐ subordinating ☐ coordinating

2 marks

2 Which coordinating conjunction completes the sentence below? Tick **one** box.

Neither Omar _____ Hannah were at school today.

☐ and ☐ for ☐ nor ☐ so

1 mark

3 Complete the sentence below using a subordinating conjunction.

We went camping _____

> Think about where, when or why you might have gone camping.

1 mark

4 a Which conjunction completes the sentence below? Tick **one** box.

They ate the dessert _____ they had finished the main course.

☐ so ☐ after ☐ until ☐ but

b Which type of conjunction is it? _____

2 marks

5 Which sentence contains a coordinating conjunction? Tick **one** box.

☐ Britain declared war on Germany in 1939 because Hitler invaded Poland.

☐ The show needs to start but the musicians aren't here!

1 mark

6 Is the statement below true or false? Tick **one** box.

Subordinating conjunctions link a main and a subordinate clause together.

☐ true ☐ false

1 mark

Time to reflect

Mark your *Have a go* section out of 8. How are you doing so far?

Check your answers in the back of the book and see how you are doing.

☐ **Had a go** 0–3 marks	☐ **Nearly there** 4–7 marks	☐ **Nailed it!** 8 marks
Have another look at the *Worked examples* on page 18. Then try these questions again.	Look at your incorrect answers. Make sure you understand how to get the correct answer.	Congratulations! Now see whether you can get full marks on the *Timed practice*.

When you are ready, try the *Timed practice* on the next page.

Timed practice

⏱ 15

1 a Underline the conjunction in the sentence below.

Dad ate two huge slices of cake although he was only supposed to have one.

b Which type of conjunction is it? Tick **one** box.

☐ subordinating   ☐ coordinating

2 marks

2 a Which conjunction completes the sentence below? Tick **one** box.

We will move into the new classroom _____ it has been decorated.

☐ yet   ☐ once   ☐ but   ☐ while

b Which type of conjunction is it?

_____

2 marks

3 Complete the sentence below using a coordinating conjunction.

Grandma would really like to go on a cruise to the Mediterranean _____ she suffers from seasickness.

1 mark

4 Which sentence contains a subordinating conjunction? Tick **one** box.

☐ There has been a change of government but living conditions haven't improved.

☐ Jan is staying at the farmhouse until 15 August.

1 mark

5 Is the statement below true or false? Tick **one** box.

Coordinating conjunctions link main clauses within a sentence.

☐ true   ☐ false

1 mark

6 Write a sentence about your favourite hobby using a subordinating conjunction.

_____

_____

1 mark

Time to reflect

Mark your *Timed practice* out of 8. How did you do?

Check your answers in the back of the book and write your score in the progress chart.

☐ *0–6 marks*
Scan the QR code for extra practice.
Then move on to the next practice section or try Test 7 in your Ten-Minute Tests book.

☐ *7–8 marks*
Well done!
Move on to the next practice section or try Test 7 in your Ten-Minute Tests book.

4 Direct Speech

Direct speech is how you report the exact words that someone says. It must be punctuated correctly to make it clear where the speech begins and ends.

Worked examples

1 Which sentence is punctuated correctly? Tick **one** box.

☐ 'Have you finished writing that story yet' asked Denise.

☐ Have you finished writing that story yet?' asked Denise.

☑ 'Have you finished writing that story yet?' asked Denise.

☐ 'Have you finished writing that story yet?' asked Denise

> The full stop is missing at the end of this sentence.

> The opening speech mark is missing.

> The question mark is missing.

abc Direct speech always has:
- speech marks at the start and end of the spoken words
- a capital letter at the start if the speech is a full sentence
- a full stop, a comma, an exclamation mark or a question mark before the closing speech mark.

Speech mark   Closing punctuation

'I won't do it!' she shouted.

Capital letter at start of spoken sentence

2 Rewrite the sentence below using the correct punctuation.

we are having dinner in the Nepalese restaurant this evening said Jean

'We are having dinner in the Nepalese restaurant this evening,' said Jean.

> Use a comma rather than a full stop at the end if the speech is followed by a reporting clause like 'said Jean'.

3 In which section is the mistake in the sentence below? Circle the correct number.

'I'm so glad you came,' / said Sangeeta, because I / couldn't have managed / without your help.'

1   ②   3   4

> Here, the speech mark before 'because' is missing.

abc When direct speech is interrupted to show who is speaking (a reporting clause), you must remember to open the speech marks again afterwards.

4 The text below has the correct punctuation but an incorrect layout. Mark the places where a new paragraph should begin using double slashes (//).

abc Start a new paragraph each time the speaker changes.

'Can I borrow your calculator?' asked Marek, 'I've forgotten mine.' //
'What, again!' exclaimed Hannah, 'That's the third time this week!' //
'It's not my fault,' mumbled Marek, 'My brother keeps taking it out of my bag.'

5 Underline all the words in the text below that should begin with capital letters.

'<u>we</u> are now arriving in the national park,' announced the tour guide from the front of the coach, '<u>if</u> you are lucky, you will soon see an alligator.'

'<u>this</u> is so exciting!' exclaimed Henri.

Beyond the exam

You don't always have to use 'said' when reporting direct speech. Think of three alternative verbs you could use for each of the situations below:
- speaking quietly
- speaking loudly.

Guided questions

1 Which sentence below is punctuated correctly? Tick **one** box.

☐ 'My tablet has stopped working' exclaimed Ali.

☐ 'My tablet has stopped working'! exclaimed Ali.

☐ 'My tablet has stopped working!' exclaimed Ali.

☐ my tablet has stopped working!' exclaimed Ali.

> Check that the punctuation is where you expect it to be. You could put a small cross where punctuation is missing to eliminate options.

2 Rewrite the sentence below using the correct punctuation.

dragons are legendary creatures that feature in many stories replied Nathan

'Dragons are _____

_____

_____

> Find the words that were actually spoken by Nathan. Remember to use:
> - a capital letter at the start of the spoken sentence
> - opening and closing speech marks
> - punctuation at the end of the spoken words
> - a full stop at the end of the sentence.

3 In which section is the mistake in the sentence below? Circle the correct number.

Aysha burst into / the room and / cried, Quick, hide! / They are coming!'

      1   2   3   4

> Direct speech can appear at any position in a sentence. Here, it is at the end of the sentence.

4 The text below has the correct punctuation, but an incorrect layout. Mark the places where a new paragraph should begin using double slashes (//).

> Look for places where the speaker changes.

'Where is everyone?' yelled Martha looking around the playground. 'I'm not sure,' replied Yasmin, 'I think they're all still in class.' 'But it's 10.30. They should be out by now,' said Martha looking around in disappointment. 'I think they have to stay in and finish their project,' replied Yasmin.

5 Underline all the words in the text below that should begin with capital letters.

'what time does the cricket match start?' asked Michael, 'we don't want to be late.'
'probably at one o'clock' answered Wayne, 'at least that's what Ivy said.'

6 Conor and his mum are talking about what they will have for dinner. Imagine three lines of their conversation and write it out using direct speech.

'Are you hungry yet, Conor?' asked Mum. _____

_____

_____

_____

Beyond the exam

Write down three questions you would like to ask someone you admire. Imagine what their answers would be. Write up your imaginary interview using direct speech.

Have a go

1 Which sentence below is punctuated correctly? Tick **one** box.

☐   Huan tiptoed up and whispered, 'Shh … the deer are behind the bush.'

☐   Huan tiptoed up and whispered, 'Shh … the deer are behind the bush'.

☐   Huan tiptoed up and whispered, 'Shh … the deer are behind the bush.

1 mark

2 Rewrite the sentence below using the correct punctuation.

after the match Ted yelled Yes we won again

> Read the sentence aloud to identify which words need to be in speech marks.

_____

_____

1 mark

3 Masa and Stephen are talking about what they did at school today. Write three lines of their conversation using direct speech.

_____

_____

_____

1 mark

4 In which section is the mistake in the sentence below? Circle the correct number.

'I went trampolining / yesterday. It / was such fun' / exclaimed Melissa.

1   2   3   4

1 mark

5 This text has the correct punctuation but incorrect layout. Mark the places where a new paragraph should begin using double slashes (//).

'I can't wait to go to the theme park next weekend,' exclaimed Bridgette. 'I'm looking forward to it too,' cried Sally, 'Which rides do you most want to go on?' 'I definitely want to go on the Red River Rapids! What about you?' 'The Space Race is my favourite.'

1 mark

6 Underline all the words in the text below that should begin with capital letters.

'this carrot cake is delicious,' said Katie, 'did you bake it yourself?'
'not completely,' admitted Aika, 'my dad helped me.'

1 mark

Time to reflect

Mark your *Have a go* section out of 6. How are you doing so far?

Check your answers in the back of the book and see how you are doing.

☐ **Had a go**
0–2 marks

☐ **Nearly there**
3–5 marks

☐ **Nailed it!**
6 marks

Have another look at the *Worked examples* on page 22. Then try these questions again.

Look at your incorrect answers. Make sure you understand how to get the correct answer.

Congratulations! Now see whether you can get full marks on the *Timed practice*.

When you are ready, try the *Timed practice* on the next page.

Timed practice

🕐 **15**

🍩 **1** Which sentence below is punctuated correctly? Tick **one** box.

☐ 'The rain is coming!' shouted the tour guide. 'Get inside quickly!'

☐ The rain is coming!' shouted the tour guide. 'Get inside quickly!'

☐ 'The rain is coming'! shouted the tour guide. 'Get inside quickly!'

1
mark

🍩 **2** Rewrite the sentence below using the correct punctuation.

where have you been demanded the teacher when we arrived ten minutes late

_____

_____

1
mark

🍩 **3** In which section is the punctuation mistake in the sentence below? Circle the correct number.

'My Grandad / is visiting this weekend and / I can't wait to see / him! cheered Rakim.

    1   2   3   4

1
mark

🍩 **4** This conversation has the correct punctuation but incorrect layout. Mark the places where a new paragraph should begin using double slashes (//).

'What are you going to do with all those blackberries,' asked Tim. 'I'm going to makes pies and jams,' replied Aunt Nancy, 'They will be delicious with cream.' 'Mmm,' replied Tim licking his lips, 'Can Mum and I come round to your house for supper soon?'

1
mark

🍩 **5** Underline all the words in the text below that should begin with capital letters.

'we are going to plant vegetables in the garden next spring,' said Julien. 'in the corner by the greenhouse.' 'will you grow carrots?' asked Sheena.

1
mark

🍩 **6** Tisha and Emma have been talking about their favourite music. Write three lines of conversation using direct speech.

_____

_____

_____

2
marks

Time to reflect

Mark your _Timed practice_ section out of 7. How did you do?

Check your answers in the back of the book and write your score in the progress chart.

☐ _0–5 marks_
Scan the QR code for extra practice.
Then move on to the next practice section or try Test 8 in your Ten-Minute Tests book.

☐ _6–7 marks_
Well done!
Move on to the next practice section or try Test 8 in your Ten-Minute Tests book.

5 Colons, semi-colons and dashes

Colons, semi-colons and dashes are used to separate parts of sentences.

Worked examples

1 Which sentence below uses a colon incorrectly? Tick **one** box.

☐ To maintain good dental hygiene you should follow these rules: avoid sweets, use a good-quality toothbrush, visit the dentist regularly and use dental floss.

☐ Émile Zola said: 'The artist is nothing without the gift, but the gift is nothing without work.'

☑ I will need to take thick socks: two fleeces, gloves, a woollen hat and a warm jacket.

> **abc** Colons are used to introduce these things:
> - lists
> - quotations
> - examples
> - explanations.

> The colon should come before 'thick socks'.

2 Punctuate the sentence below with a semi-colon.

Wales is an interesting place to visit ; a lot of coal mining used to go on there.

> **abc** Semi-colons are used to separate these things:
> - two main clauses
> - complex items in a list.

> A semi-colon is used because the two clauses are about the same topic and are of equal importance.

3 Rewrite the sentence below using semi-colons.

I love everything about Liverpool: the wide, fast-flowing river the splendid, towering buildings the docks and the museums.

I love everything about Liverpool: the wide, fast-flowing river;

the splendid, towering buildings; the docks and the museums.

> **abc** Semi-colons are used in lists instead of commas if the items in the list already include punctuation. This makes the meaning of the list clearer.

4 Punctuate the sentence below using a dash.

I hope you can come to the park – there's a match on today.

> **abc** Dashes are used instead of colons to add extra information in more informal writing.

5 Rewrite the sentence below using colons and semi-colons.

There is a lot of lovely food to eat in Italy juicy, ripe peaches rich chocolate desserts creamy pasta and delicious cheese.

There is a lot of lovely food to eat in Italy: juicy, ripe peaches;

rich chocolate desserts; creamy pasta; and delicious cheese.

> The colon is used to introduce the list and semi-colons are used to separate the items in the list (because the items themselves include commas in their description).

> **abc** If you use semi-colons to punctuate a list, you must add a semi-colon before the final item.

Guided questions

1 Which sentence below is punctuated correctly? Tick **one** box.

☐ The famous inventor Thomas Edison: once said 'I've not failed. I've just found 10 000 ways that won't work.'

☐ The famous inventor Thomas Edison once said: 'I've not failed. I've just found 10 000 ways that won't work.'

☐ The famous inventor Thomas Edison once said 'I've not failed: I've just found 10 000 ways that won't work.

☐ The famous inventor: Thomas Edison once said: 'I've not failed. I've just found 10 000 ways that won't work.'

> Read each sentence carefully, marking any incorrect or missing punctuation with a cross. This will help you eliminate the wrong answers.

2 Punctuate the sentence below with a colon.

> The colon should go between the main clause and the subordinate clause.

When making meringue you should always whip the egg whites until they are stiff if you don't the mixture won't rise.

3 Rewrite the sentence below using a semi-colon.

> The two main clauses are of equal importance and linked by topic.

Dromedary camels have one hump Bactrian camels have two humps.

_____

4 Complete the sentence using a colon, semi-colon or dash.

I love reading science fiction stories _____ they really make me think.

> The second clause provides further explanation of the first. This helps you choose which punctuation to use.

5 Write a sentence including a list, using at least one colon and either commas or semi-colons.

On Mum's birthday we will _____

_____

6 Punctuate the sentence below.

> Try counting the items on your fingers as you read the list.

You will have a great choice of activities at the camp windsurfing hiking up magnificent, heather-covered hillsides canoeing around the huge, blue lake and swimming.

7 True or false? Tick **one** box.

> Go back to page 26 for a reminder of when to use dashes.

Dashes can be used instead of colons in informal language.

☐ true   ☐ false

Beyond the exam

Invent a hand sign to represent colons and another to represent semi colons. For example:

- one hand in a fist = colon
- two hands in fists = semi colon.

With a partner, each write five sentences using colons and semi colons.

Ask your partner to sign the punctuation as you read your sentences to them. Then swap over.

Have a go

1 Which sentence is punctuated correctly? Tick **one** box.

1 mark

☐ Many crops are grown on the farm: butternut squash to name one.

☐ Many crops: are grown on the farm butternut squash to name one.

☐ Many crops are grown on the farm butternut squash: to name one.

2 Punctuate the sentence below using a colon.

1 mark

> Vivien Greene famously said 'Life isn't about waiting for the storm to pass, it's about dancing in the rain.'

3 Punctuate the sentence below using a semi-colon. • ─────

1 mark

> **Think about where one clause ends and another begins.**

> Most tea is produced in China most coffee comes from Brazil.

4 Rewrite the sentence below using semi-colons to punctuate the list.

> I dislike everything about that café: the cold, burnt toasties the horrible, uncomfortable chairs the bad music and the rude owner.

1 mark

_____

_____

5 You are planning a birthday party. Write a sentence with a list of items you need, using at least one colon and either commas or semi-colons.

2 marks

_____

_____

6 Rewrite the sentence below using the correct punctuation.

> I have so much homework to do this weekend a long, tedious history essay two pages of difficult French exercises and some geography.

abc 'Tedious' means 'boring'.

2 marks

_____

_____

_____

Time to reflect

Mark your *Have a go* section out of 8. How are you doing so far?

Check your answers in the back of the book and see how you are doing.

☐ **Had a go**
0–4

Have another look at the *Worked examples* on page 26. Then try these questions again.

☐ **Nearly there**
5–7 marks

Look at your incorrect answers. Make sure you understand how to get the correct answer.

☐ **Nailed it!**
8 marks

Congratulations! Now see whether you can get full marks on the *Timed practice*.

When you are ready, try the *Timed practice* on the next page.

Timed practice

🕐 **15**

1 Which sentence below is punctuated correctly? Tick one box.

☐ She's not coming: to the party she's got the flu.

☐ She's not coming to the party she's got the flu.

☐ She's not coming to the party: she's got the flu.

☐ She's not coming: to the party she's got the flu.

1 mark

2 Punctuate the sentence below with a semi-colon.

The days are very short in winter they are very long in summer.

1 mark

3 Punctuate the sentence below with a colon.

The friends were totally exhausted they had walked fifteen miles.

1 mark

4 Rewrite the sentence below, using semi-colons to punctuate the list.

Dad's special salad recipe includes: fresh, free-range eggs delicious, salty olives crisp lettuce and ripe cherry tomatoes.

_____

_____

_____

1 mark

5 Complete the sentence below using either a colon, semi-colon or dash.

I can't believe he said that _____ it was so funny!

1 mark

6 You are going on a trip to the desert. Write a sentence with a list of items you need to pack, using at least one colon and either commas or semi-colons.

_____

_____

1 mark

7 Is the statement below true or false? Tick **one** box.

Semi-colons are used to introduce a quotation.

☐ true   ☐ false

1 mark

Time to reflect

Mark your *Timed practice* out of 7. How did you do?

Check your answers in the back of the book and write your score in the progress chart.

☐ *0–5 marks*
Scan the QR code for extra practice.
Then move on to the next practice section or try Test 9 in your Ten-Minute Tests book.

☐ *6–7 marks*
Well done!
Move on to the next practice section or try Test 9 in your Ten-Minute Tests book

6 Apostrophes

Apostrophes are used to show missing letters in contractions and to show possession.

Worked examples

1 Rewrite the sentence below using two contractions.

I do not think they will arrive in time for the start of the concert.

I don't think they'll arrive in time for the start of the concert.

> **abc** A contraction is made of two or more words joined together with some letters missed out to make it easier to say. You replace the missing letters with an apostrophe. For example, I am = I'm.

> In this sentence 'do not' has been replaced with 'don't' and 'they will' with 'they'll'.

2 Which sentence below is correctly punctuated? Tick **one** box.

☐ William Shakespeares plays are famous throughout the world.

☑ William Shakespeare's plays are famous throughout the world.

☐ William Shakespeares' plays are famous throughout the world.

☐ William Shakespear'es plays are famous throughout the world.

> **abc** To show possession add an apostrophe and **s**.

> If the subject has more than one name, you only need to put the apostrophe at the end of the last name.

3 Punctuate the sentence below using a possessive apostrophe.

The childrens playground has swings and a slide.

The children's playground has swings and slide.

4 Circle the correct spelling in the sentence below.

The lorry trundled down the road, fumes pouring out of **its'** / **it's** / (**its**) exhaust.

> **abc** Remember these rules:
> - it's = it is (contraction)
> - its = possessive pronoun (like 'his' or 'her')

> Here 'its' is a possessive pronoun because the exhaust belongs to the lorry.

> **abc**
> - For **regular plurals** (that end in 's', for example, boys) add the apostrophe **after** the s.
>   The toilet belonging to the boys = the boys' toilet.
> - For **irregular plurals** (that don't end in 's', for example, children) add an apostrophe and s.
>   The playground belonging to the children = the children's playground.

5 Rewrite the sentence below using an apostrophe.

The books belonging to Charles are in the cupboard.

Charles's books are in the cupboard.

> You may need to rearrange the words to show possession.

6 Rewrite the sentence below using a contraction in place of the underlined word.

Although Kali's bedroom looks good, she says <u>she will</u> redecorate it soon.

Although Kali's bedroom looks good, she says she'll redecorate it soon.

7 Write a sentence about something a member of your family owns, using a possessive apostrophe.

My brother's hamster is very cute.

Guided questions

1 Rewrite the sentence below using two contractions.

We will be able to find out who is coming from the guest list.

> Read the sentence aloud to see which words you should shorten.

_____

_____

2 Which sentence below is correctly punctuated? Tick **one** box.

☐　The ladies' changing room is on the far side of the sports centre.

> The plural noun is 'ladies'.

☐　The ladie's changing room is one the far side of the sports centre.

☐　The ladies changing room is on the far side of the sports' centre.

☐　The ladi'es changing room is on the far side of the sports centre.

3 Punctuate the sentence below using a possessive apostrophe.

My mums car is really old.

> Think about who owns the car.

4 Rewrite the sentence below using a possessive apostrophe.

The handle on the cooker has fallen off.

> The handle belongs to the cooker.

_____

_____

5 In which section is the mistake in the sentence below? Circle the correct number.

The other player's / shot just missed / the goal so Mandys / team won after all.

> Try to work out who things belong to in the sentence.

1　　　　　2　　　　　3　　　　　4

6 Write a sentence about something the students in your school own (for example books), using a possessive apostrophe.

> Remember to include the plural noun 'students' and put the possessive apostrophe in the correct place.

_____

_____

7 Is the statement below true or false? Tick **one** box.

You should add a possessive apostrophe to 'its' to show possession.

> Remember: 'it's' (with an apostrophe) is a contraction of 'it is'.

☐　true　　　☐　false

Beyond the exam

Find two old newspaper articles of equal length. Highlight examples of possessive apostrophes with a partner. Who can find the most in five minutes?

Have a go

1 Rewrite the sentence below using a contraction.

Do not take drinks into the classroom.

_____

_____

1 mark

2 Which sentence below is correctly punctuated? Tick **one** box.

☐ He'wll need to get more paint to finish the painting.

☐ He'll need to get more paint to finish the painting.

☐ H'ell need to get more paint to finish the painting.

1 mark

> In contractions the apostrophe replaces missing letters.

3 Punctuate the sentence below using a possessive apostrophe.

The womens business is a great success.

1 mark

> Go to page 30 to revise using possessive apostrophes with irregular plurals.

4 Circle the correct spelling in brackets in the sentence below.

The boys will race this afternoon but the (girl's / girls / girls') race will start now.

1 mark

5 Rewrite the sentence below using a possessive apostrophe.

The book belonging to Joshua is in his bag.

_____

_____

1 mark

6 In which section is the punctuation mistake in the sentence below? Circle the correct number.

Florence Nightingale's / legacy remains / in our nursing system / and it's philosophy of care.

1   2   3   4

1 mark

7 Rewrite the sentence below using a contraction to replace the underlined words.

<u>She would</u> love it there – the scenery is beautiful.

_____

_____

1 mark

> Read the sentence aloud to hear the contraction.

Time to reflect

Mark your *Have a go* section out of 7. How are you doing so far?

Check your answers in the back of the book and see how you are doing.

☐ **Had a go**
0–4 marks

Have another look at the *Worked examples* on page 30. Then try these questions again.

☐ **Nearly there**
5–6 marks

Look at your incorrect answers. Make sure you understand how to get the correct answer.

☐ **Nailed it!**
7 marks

Congratulations! Now see whether you can get full marks on the *Timed practice.*

When you are ready, try the *Timed practice* on the next page.

Timed practice

⏱ **15**

1 Rewrite the sentence below using a contraction.

I have not been to Blackpool for ages.

_____

_____

`1` mark

2 Which sentence below is correctly punctuated? Tick **one** box.

☐ The torches's beams shone on their startled faces.   ☐ The torche's beams shone on their startled faces.

☐ The torches' beams shone on their startled faces.   ☐ The torch'es beams shone on their startled faces.

`1` mark

3 Punctuate the sentence below using a possessive apostrophe.

The dancers costumes looked fantastic.

`1` mark

4 Circle the correct spelling in brackets in the sentence below.

Henry (should'ave / should've / shouldv'e) arrived in New York by now.

`1` mark

5 Rewrite the sentence below using a possessive apostrophe.

The tractor belonging to the farmer is extremely muddy.

_____

_____

`1` mark

6 In which section is the mistake in the sentence below? Circle the correct number.

The plants leaves / are very lush /even though its / flowers have died.

1   2   3   4

`1` mark

7 Rewrite the sentence below using a contraction to replace the underlined words.

Sunil paid a lot for his phone; he <u>could have</u> saved money if <u>he had</u> shopped around.

_____

_____

`1` mark

8 Write a sentence about something your neighbours own, using a possessive apostrophe.

_____

_____

`1` mark

Time to reflect

Mark your *Timed practice* section out of 8. How did you do?

Check your answers in the back of the book and write your score in the progress chart.

☐ *0–6 marks*
Scan the QR code for extra practice.
Then move on to the next practice section or
try Test 10 in your Ten-Minute Tests book.

☐ *7–8 marks*
Well done!
Move on to the next practice section or try Test 10
in your Ten-Minute Tests book.

Checkpoint 1

In this checkpoint you will practise skills from the **Grammar and punctuation** topic.

(15)

1 Punctuate the parenthesis in this sentence using dashes.

Section 1

If our team wins the match on Saturday and everyone thinks they will we will go and watch the final next month.

1 mark

2 Which sentence is punctuated correctly? Tick **one** box.

Section 6

☐ The firemens's helmets are designed to protect them from heat and falling cinders.

☐ The firemen's helmets are designed to protect them from heat and falling cinders.

☐ The firemens' helmets are designed to protect them from heat and falling cinders.

1 mark

3 Rewrite the following sentence using the correct punctuation.

Section 4

My favourite films are action movies said Joshua.

_____

_____

1 mark

4 Which preposition of place completes the sentence below? Tick **one** box.

Section 2

The post office is situated _____ the newsagents and the laundrette.

☐ between

☐ on

☐ in

☐ at

1 mark

5 Which sentence is punctuated correctly? Tick **one** box.

Section 5

☐ To avoid catching colds and spreading germs you should always wash: your hands before eating, put used tissues in the bin and never share cups with other people.

☐ To avoid catching colds and spreading germs you should always wash your hands before eating: put used tissues in the bin and never share cups with other people.

☐ To avoid catching colds and spreading germs you should always: wash your hands before eating, put used tissues in the bin and never share cups with other people

1 mark

6 In which section is the mistake? Circle the correct number.

Section 1

River otters (semiaquatic / mammals are) / also carnivores as / they eat fish.

1   2   3   4

1 mark

7 Rewrite the following sentence with the correct punctuation.

Section 4

The cruise ship has now docked in the port announced Mr Wilson.

_____

_____

_____

1 mark

8 Which type of conjunction are the following conjunctions? Tick **one** box.

Section 3

	coordinating	subordinating
because	☐	☐
while	☐	☐
nor	☐	☐
but	☐	☐

2 marks

9 Is the statement below true or false? Tick **one** box.

Section 6

You should not add a possessive apostrophe to 'its' to show ownership.

☐ true

☐ false

1 mark

Time to reflect

Mark your *Checkpoint* out of 10. How did you do?

1 Check your answers in the back of the book and write your score in the progress chart.
If any of your answers are incorrect, use the section links to find out which practice sections to look at again.

2 Scan the QR code for extra practice.

3 Move on to the next practice section.

7 Homophones and homonyms

Homophones are words that sound the same or very similar but have different spellings. Homonyms are words that are spelled the same but have different meanings.

Worked examples

1 Underline the correct homophone in each of the sentences below.

   a Tulips are mum's favourite (<u>flower</u> / flour).

   b It is wrong to (<u>steal</u> / steel).

   c I have to (practice / <u>practise</u>) the piano this evening.

2 Underline the correct homophone in brackets the sentence below.

   Our car is blue but (there's / <u>theirs</u>) is silver.

3 Complete the sentences below using these homophones.

   bored   board

   a I am really <u>bored</u> with watching TV.

   b Can we play a <u>board</u> game?

4 The word 'match' is a homonym. It can mean a game of football ('Tom went to the match.') Write a definition of another of its meanings.

A match is a very small stick of wood that you strike to make a flame.

5 Write two sentences including the homophones below.

   knight   night

   1 The knight bravely fought the dragon.

   2 The barn owl hunts at night.

6 Is the statement below true or false? Tick **one** box.

   Homophones are words that sound the same and have the same spelling.

   ☐ true
   ☑ false

---

abc Homophones are words that sound the same but have different spellings. For example:
- Can I have a **piece** of cake?
- The dove is a symbol of **peace**.

abc Some homophones are different word classes. The suffix **-ice** is usually used for nouns (practice) and the suffix **-ise** is usually used for verbs (practise).

'There's' is a contraction meaning 'there is'.

abc Homonyms are words that are spelled the same but have different meanings. For example:
- The black **bear** is native to America.
- I can't **bear** my big brother!

abc
- 'Homo' is the ancient Greek word for 'same'.
- 'Phone' means 'sound'.
- 'Nym' means 'name'.

Guided questions

1 Underline the correct homophone in each of the sentences below.

  a All the (patients / patience) were waiting in the doctor's waiting room.

  b Moses was an Egyptian prince who became a (profit / prophet).

  c If I am ever worried, my grandpa gives me helpful (advice / advise).

> Think about the meaning of the word in the context of the sentence.

> **abc** A prophet is an important religious person who speaks the word of God.

2 The sentence below uses the homonym 'pound'.
Write a sentence using the alternative meaning of 'pound'.

    Jacob has taken up running and is always pounding the pavements.

> Decide whether the correct word is a noun or a verb and choose the correct suffix to show this.

The school trip costs

3 Underline the correct homophone in brackets the sentence below.

    The teacher asked (whose / who's) jacket had been left on the floor.

> Expand the contraction 'who's' to 'who is' or 'who has' and check whether it makes sense in the sentence.

4 Complete the sentences below using these homophones.

  main   mane

  a I am auditioning for a _____ part in the play.

> Read the sentences carefully and think about the meaning of both homophones.

  b The huge lion has an enormous, scraggy _____.

6 Write two separate sentences, each using the homonym 'bark' in a different way.

> Remember, the two meanings might be different parts of speech.

  1 _____

  _____

  2 _____

  _____

Beyond the exam

With a partner make a set of ten cards with one homophone on each.
For example:
- beech / beach
- made / maid
- cheap / cheep

Put the cards face down on the table. Take turns to choose a card and make up a sentence with the word on the card in it.

Have a go

1 Underline the correct homophone in each of the sentences below.

    a The (loan / lone) traveller made his way down the dusty road.

    b You are not (aloud /allowed) to use your phone during lessons.

    c We need to (devise / device) a better way of transporting the bicycles.

3 marks

2 The word 'rose' is a homonym. It can be the name for a type of flower. Write a definition of another of its meanings.

1 mark

_____

3 Underline the correct homophone in the sentence below.

    I enjoyed the (descent / dissent) down the mountain the most.

> One of these homophones means 'to disagree', the other means to move downwards.

1 mark

4 Complete the sentences below using these homophones.

    stares   stairs

    a The boy stands and _____ at the beautiful view.

    b Go up the _____ to the x-ray clinic.

2 marks

5 Write two sentences including the homophones below.

    principal   principle

> One of these homophones means 'the most important'. The other is a name for the head of a school or college.

    1 _____

    2 _____

2 marks

6 Is the statement below true or false? Tick **one** box.

    Homonyms are words that sound the same but are spelled the differently.

    ☐ true   ☐ false

> Remember the meanings of the ancient Greek root words: 'homo', 'phone' and 'nym'.

1 mark

Time to reflect

Mark your *Have a go* section out of 10. How are you doing so far?

Check your answers in the back of the book and see how you are doing.

☐ **Had a go**	☐ **Nearly there**	☐ **Nailed it!**
0–5 marks	*6–9 marks*	*10 marks*
Have another look at the *Worked examples* on page 36. Then try these questions again.	Look at your incorrect answers. Make sure you understand how to get the correct answer.	Congratulations! Now see whether you can get full marks on the *Timed practice*.

When you are ready, try the *Timed practice* on the next page.

Timed practice

⏱ **15**

1 Underline the correct homophone in each of the sentences below.

   a Uma likes toast for breakfast but I prefer (serial / cereal).

   b The Prince is the (air / heir) to the throne.

   c My sister has applied for her provisional driving (licence / license).

3 marks

2 The word 'address' is a homonym. It can mean 'to speak to person or group of people'. Write a definition of another of its meanings.

_____

1 mark

3 Underline the correct homophone in the sentence below.

     We will know when (they're / there) coming because we will hear them.

1 mark

4 Complete the sentences below using these homophones.

   mourning   morning

   a I'll phone you in the _____ .

   b Howard's great grandfather died yesterday so his whole family is in _____ .

2 marks

5 Write two sentences including the homophones below.

   blue   blew

   1 _____

      _____

   2 _____

      _____

2 marks

7 Is the statement below true or false? Tick **one** box.

     Homophones are always spelled differently.

   ☐ true   ☐ false

1 mark

Time to reflect

Mark your *Timed practice* section out of 10. How did you do?

Check your answers in the back of the book and write your score in the progress chart.

   ☐ *0–8 marks*
   Scan the QR code for extra practice.
Then move on to the next practice section or try Test 14 in your Ten-Minute Tests book.

   ☐ *9–10 marks*
   Well done!
Move on to the next practice section or try Test 14 in your Ten-Minute Tests book.

8 ie/ei and ough spellings

The letter strings **ie** or **ei** can both represent the sound /ee/. The letter string **ough** represents seven different sounds. Make sure you learn these tricky spellings.

Worked examples

1 Circle the correct spelling below.

  a (receipt)/ reciept

  b yeild /(yield)

> **abc** Remember the rule: when the sound is /ee/, use **i** before **e** except after **c**.

2 Complete the sentence below using **ie** or **ei**.

    It was dec___*ei*___tful of him to steal the money.

3 Read the definition below and complete word with **ie** or **ei**.

    An important religious person in the Catholic church: pr___*ie*___st

> Check whether the word contains the letter **c**.

4 Which word below rhymes with 'kangaroo'? Tick **one** box.

  ☐ enough

  ☐ ought

  ☑ through

> **abc** The letter string **ough** is used to represent seven different sounds. For example: plough, cough, though, through, rough, ought, borough.

5 Write an 'ough' word that means the opposite of smooth.

    rough

6 In which section is the spelling mistake in the sentence below? Circle the correct number.

    He taught martial arts / in Loughborough / which is a town in / the borugh of Charnwood.

    1   2   3   (4)

> The correct spelling is 'borough', which means an area of the country.

Beyond the exam

Make a flash card for each of the words below. With a partner, take turns picking a card and saying as many words that rhyme with it as possible in ten seconds.

- rough
- bought
- cough
- though
- through
- plough
- thorough

Guided questions

1 Circle the correct spelling in each of the pairs below.

    a achievement / acheivement ●──────────

    b conceived / concieved

> A **c** only changes the order of the **ie** if it comes immediately before it and makes the /ee/ sound.

2 Complete the sentence below using **ie** or **ei**.

    The meadows and f_____lds are full of beautiful, wild flowers.

3 Read the definition below and complete the word using **ie** or **ei**.

    A shelf of wood or stone over a fireplace: mantelp_____ce ●───────

> Look carefully at where the **c** is.

4 Which word below has an **ough** sound that rhymes with 'or'? Tick **one** box. ●───────

> In **ough** words that end in **t**, the **ough** sound always rhymes with 'or'.

    ☐ thorough

    ☐ sought

    ☐ though

5 Write an **ough** word for bread mixture before it is baked.

d_____

6 In which section is the spelling mistake in the sentence below? Circle the correct number.

> Some **ough** words rhyme with 'off'.

    Even though she / kept warm she / caught a bad cogh / and a heavy cold.

       1   2   3   4

7 Write a sentence using the '**i** before **e**' rule about getting a letter in the post.

Yesterday I _____

_____

8 Write an **ough** word that is the past tense of the verb 'fight'

f_____

Have a go

1 Circle the correct spelling in each of the pairs below.

2 marks

    a conceited   concieted

    b neice   niece

> Go to page 40 to revise the rule about **ie** and **ei** words with a **c**.

2 Complete the sentence below using **ie** or **ei**.

1 mark

      My little brother is full of misch_____f and always playing tricks.

3 Read the definition below and complete the word using **ie** or **ei**.

1 mark

      When something has a short duration: br_____f

4 Write the plural of the word below.

      baby

1 mark

      _____

5 Which word below rhymes with 'puff'? Tick **one** box.

      ☐ enough

      ☐ nought

1 mark

      ☐ although

> Remember, **ough** can be pronounced in seven different ways. Go to page 40 to see examples of the sounds.

6 Write an **ough** word that means 'to dig up a field in order to plant crops'

1 mark

      _____

7 In which section is the spelling mistake in the sentence below? Write the correct number.

      Although he boght / plenty of food everything / was eaten by / the end of the day.

1 mark

         1   2   3   4

8 Is the statement below true or false? Tick **one** box.

      In all words, **i** comes before **e** except after **c**.

1 mark

      ☐ true   ☐ false

Time to reflect

Mark your *Have a go* section out of 9. How are you doing so far?

Check your answers in the back of the book and see how you are doing.

☐ **Had a go**
0–4 marks

☐ **Nearly there**
5–8 marks

☐ **Nailed it!**
9 marks

Have another look at the *Worked examples* on page 40. Then try these questions again.

Look at your incorrect answers. Make sure you understand how to get the correct answer.

Congratulations! Now see whether you can get full marks on the *Timed practice*.

When you are ready, try the *Timed practice* on the next page.

Timed practice

⏱ **15**

1 Circle the correct spelling in the pairs below.

   a perceive / percieve

   b relief / releif

2
marks

2 Complete the sentence below using **ei** or **ie**.

   Before a race, athletes must eat food that is high in calor_____s.

1
mark

3 Read the definition below and complete the word using **ie** or **ei**.

   Someone who steals things: th_____

1
mark

4 Which word below has an **ough** sound that rhymes with 'so'? Tick **one** box.

   ☐ brought   ☐ though   ☐ cough

1
mark

5 In which section is the spelling mistake in the sentence below? Circle the correct number.

   Having given this / a lot of thourt / I've decided that / the best plan is to get the bus.

   1   2   3   4

1
mark

6 Complete the sentence below using an **ei** or **ie** word.

   I had a _____ of chocolate cake for dessert.

1
mark

7 Is the statement below true or false? Tick **one** box.

   The letter string **ough** sometimes represents the sound /or/.

   ☐ true   ☐ false

1
mark

8 a Write a sentence about a shopping trip using an **ough** word.

   _____

   b Write a word that rhymes with the **ough** word in your sentence above.

   _____

2
marks

Time to reflect

Mark your *Timed practice* section out of 10. How did you do?

Check your answers in the back of the book and write your score in the progress chart.

☐ *0–8 marks*
Scan the QR code for extra practice.
Then move on to the next practice section or
try Test 15 in your Ten-Minute Tests book.

☐ *9–10 marks*
Well done!
Move on to the next practice section or try Test 15
in your Ten-Minute Tests book.

9 Tricky spellings

You sometimes need to double the final letter of a root word when you add a suffix. Make sure you know the two main rules for this. Watch out for words with unstressed sounds, as these can be tricky to spell too.

Worked examples

1 Read the definition below and complete the word.

A place where people can borrow books: library

2 Complete the sentence below by adding a suffix to the root word 'stop'.

The rain has finally stopped.

3 Which word below is spelled correctly? Tick **one** box.

☐ embarrasing

☐ embarasing

☐ embarrassing

4 What are the measurements below all examples of?

3 °C   −10 °C   21 °C

temperatures

5 Complete the word below.

gover n ment

6 Which sentence below is spelled correctly? Tick **one** box.

☐ I liked the suspense at the begining of the story.

☐ I liked the suspense at the beginning of the story.

☐ I liked the suspense at the begginning of the story.

☐ I liked the suspense at the beginin of the story.

7 Complete the sentence below by adding a suffix to the root word 'rub'.

Has anyone seen my rubber?

abc Stress is how clearly or unclearly the sounds in a word are said. Unstressed sounds are not heard very clearly when you say a word out loud (the 'r' in 'library', for example), so you must be careful when spelling them.

abc If the root word is one syllable and ends in a consonant-vowel-consonant pattern, you double the final letter before you add the suffix. Go to Practice Section 5 in Practice Book 1 for more about adding suffixes.

In this example, 'embarrass' is the root and **-ing** is the suffix.

abc If the root word already has double letters, you keep them when you add the suffix.

The second **e** in 'temperature' is unstressed.

In this example, a consonant is unstressed.

abc When adding a suffix to a root word that has more than one syllable and ends with a consonant, look at which syllable is stressed. If the last syllable is stressed, you must double the final consonant.

Beyond the exam

Make a list of ten words with more than one syllable.

Practise saying them aloud and clapping on the stressed sounds.

Guided questions

1 Which word below is spelled correctly? Tick **one** box.

☐ secret
☐ secrit
☐ seecrut
☐ secrot

> Sometimes a vowel might be pronounced to sound like another vowel.

2 Complete the sentence below by adding a suffix to the root word 'marvel'.

The new series is _____?

> Say the root word aloud to work out which syllable is stressed.

3 In which section is the spelling mistake? Circle the correct number.

> Look for a word with an unstressed vowel.

The charity workers / made a hazardous journey / to deliver vital / medcine and supplies.

1 2 3 4

4 Complete the word below.

g__arantee

> Think about how the word 'guard' is spelled and said.

5 Which of the sentences below is spelled correctly? Tick **one** box.

☐ I refferred to an atlas to help with my homework.
☐ I refered to an atlas to help with my homework.
☐ I refferd to an atlas to help with my homework.
☐ I referred to an atlas to help with my homework.

> **abc** If the suffix you are adding to a root word begins with a consonant, you don't need to double the final letter.

6 Complete the sentence below by adding a suffix to the root word 'sad'.

_____, my best friend couldn't come to the party.

7 In which section is the mistake? Circle the correct number.

My cousin is / planning a / truly spectacular / weding.

1 2 3 4

> Look for a root word with a consonant-vowel-consonant pattern.

Beyond the exam

With a partner, use a dictionary to find six polysyllabic words (words with more than one syllable).

Write each word on a piece of paper and cut them into separate syllables.

Take it in turns to jumble a word up.

Ask your partner to rearrange the word to form the correct spelling.

Have a go

1 Read the definition below and complete the word.

2 marks

   a An adjective to describe something scary: fr_____

   b A place where you can go to eat food: r_____

2 Which sentence below is spelled correctly? Tick **one** box.

1 mark

  ☐ Rajesh is always the winner when we play boardgames.

  ☐ Rajesh is always the winer when we play boardgames.

  ☐ Rajesh is always the winneer when we play boardgames.

  ☐ Rajesh is always the winerr when we play boardgames.

> Look closely at each word in turn and think about whether it looks correct.

3 In which section is the spelling mistake? Circle the correct number.

1 mark

When I travel abroad / I really appreciate being / able to speak another / languige.

       1   2   3   4

4 What are all the items below used for?

1 mark

scissors   knife   shears   saw

1 mark

_____ing

5 Complete the word: enviro_____ment

1 mark

> To form the past tense you need to add a suffix to a root word. Think about whether you need to double any letters.

6 Complete the sentence below using a past tense verb.

1 mark

My sister an_____ the phone.

7 Complete the sentence below.

1 mark

My little sister's favourite puzzle is spot the d_____.

8 Write a sentence including an adverb made by adding a suffix to the adjective 'mad'.

> Check whether the suffix begins with a vowel or a consonant.

1 mark

_____

_____

Time to reflect

Mark your *Have a go* section out of 9. How are you doing so far?

Check your answers in the back of the book and see how you are doing.

☐ **Had a go**
0–4 marks

☐ **Nearly there**
5–8 marks

☐ **Nailed it!**
9 marks

Have another look at the *Worked examples* on page 44. Then try these questions again.

Look at your incorrect answers. Make sure you understand how to get the correct answer.

Congratulations! Now see whether you can get full marks on the *Timed practice*.

When you are ready, try the *Timed practice* on the next page.

Timed practice

⏱ **15**

1 Read the definition below and complete the word.

An office worker who deals with paper work and answers the telephone: s_____

1 mark

2 Which word below is spelled correctly? Tick **one** box.

☐ corresponddding ☐ correspondin ☐ corresponding ☐ correspnding

1 mark

3 Complete the sentences below using present progressive tense verbs.

a 'Ouch,' cried Dad, rub _____ his toe.

b We've been plan _____ the trip for ages.

2 marks

4 Which sentence below is spelled correctly? Tick **one** box.

☐ After he was caught cheating, he was ommited from the competition.

☐ After he was caught cheating, he was omitted from the competition.

☐ After he was caught cheating, he was omited from the competition.

☐ After he was caught cheating, he was ommitted from the competition.

1 mark

5 In which section is the spelling mistake? Circle the correct number.

My teacher recommendded / that we look up / unfamiliar words / in a dictionary.

1   2   3   4

1 mark

6 What are the items below examples of?

carrots   potatoes   cabbage   broccoli

_____

1 mark

7 Add a suffix to the adjective to form an adverb: bad_____

1 mark

8 Complete the sentence below with the past tense of the verb 'finish'.

Can I have desert now I've _____ my dinner?

1 mark

9 Read the definition below and complete the word.

A musical instrument with six strings, often used in rock music: g_____

1 mark

Time to reflect

Mark your *Timed practice* section out of 10. How did you do?

Check your answers in the back of the book and write your score in the progress chart.

☐ *0–8 marks*
Scan the QR code for extra practice.
Then move on to the next practice section or try Test 16 in your Ten-Minute Tests book.

☐ *9–10 marks*
Well done!
Move on to the next practice section or try Test 16 in your Ten-Minute Tests book.

Checkpoint 2

In this checkpoint you will practise skills from the **Spelling** topic

(15)

1 Circle the correct homophone in brackets in the sentence below.

Section 7

1 mark

The early morning (missed / mist) hung over the valley.

2 Underline the correct spelling in brackets in the sentence below.

Section 8

1 mark

The car takes (diesel / deisel) not petrol.

3 Which sentence is spelled correctly? Tick **one** box.

Section 7

☐ I think it would be interesting to go and live abroad in a foriegn country.

☐ I think it would be interesting to go and live abroad in a foreign country.

☐ I think it would be interesting to go and live abroad in a foregn country.

☐ I think it would be interesting to go and live abroad in a forign country.

1 mark

4 In which section is the mistake? Circle the correct number.

Section 9

1 mark

Although she was trying / to help, she was actually / a hinderence because/ she kept interrupting everyone.

    1   2   3   4

5 Rewrite the following sentence with the correct spelling of the word in brackets.

Section 9

It isn't really (neccessarry) to wear hiking boots because it's only a short walk.

1 mark

_____

_____

_____

6 Write two sentences that include the following homonyms.

Section 7

spring   spring

1 _____

_____

2 _____

2 marks

_____

7 Is the statement below true or false? Tick **one** box.

Section 7

Homophones are words which sound the same but have different meanings.

☐ true

☐ false

1 mark

8 Which is the correct spelling? Tick **one** box..

Section 9

☐ enviroment

☐ envonment

☐ environment

☐ environnment

1
mark

9 Circle the correct homophone in brackets.

Section 7

1
mark

We went to the (stationary / stationery) shop to buy writing paper and envelopes.

10 Underline the correct spelling in brackets in the sentence below.

Section 8

1
mark

The tyres of this jeep are very (tough / tuff) and made for off-road conditions.

11 Which is the correct spelling? Tick **one** box.

Section 9

☐ commpetition

☐ compertition

☐ competition

☐ competion

1
mark

12 Underline the correct spelling in brackets in the sentence below.

Section 8

1
mark

Would you like another (peice / piece) of cake?

Time to reflect

Mark your *Checkpoint* out of 13. How did you do?

1 Check your answers in the back of the book and write your score in the progress chart.
If any of your answers are incorrect, use the section links to find out which practice sections to look at again.

2 Scan the QR code for extra practice.

3 Move on to the next practice section.

10 Understanding texts

Some comprehension questions may ask you to explain the meaning of particular words or phrases. You may also be asked to explain how a text is structured and why.

Worked examples

This extract is from a nature magazine.

Brilliant Bolving

Do you know what 'bolving' is? I didn't until very recently. 'Bolving' is an activity where people impersonate a stag. Now, this doesn't mean that bolving participants run around on all fours wearing antlers and mimicking a deer! The only thing that they try to replicate is the sound a stag makes when calling to other deer during the rutting (mating) season. This is a very loud bellowing that sounds rather like the hybrid of a lion roaring and a cow mooing. The stag does this to demonstrate how strong he is and to frighten off other stags who want to take over his herd.

A stag's bellow is a very challenging noise for a human to make, but that doesn't deter the bolving participants. Annual championships take place in Exmoor in Devon, the Peak District in Derbyshire and the Scottish Highlands.

1 a The writer opens this text with a question. Why do you think this is? Tick **one** box.

- [ ] because the writer doesn't know what bolving is and wants to find out
- [x] to get the reader interested in reading more
- [ ] so that only those who know the answer will keep reading

abc **Structure** refers to how a text is organised. For example, how it begins and ends, what tense it is written in and how it is divided into paragraphs.

2 Explain in your own words why the writer uses a new paragraph for the section beginning 'A stag's bellow'.

The author uses a new paragraph when they change topic to the bolving championships.

abc A writer should start a new paragraph when they talk about a new person, place or topic, or when the story moves forwards or backwards in time. Go to Practice Section 13 in Practice Book 1 for more about paragraphs.

3 Find and copy two words in the text that mean 'copying'.

1   mimicking

2   impersonating

Check whether you have found the right word in the text by replacing it with the word in the question. If it fits without changing the meaning of the sentence, it is probably correct.

4 What does 'hybrid' mean? Tick **one** box.

- [ ] It is a type of deer.
- [ ] It is a way of saying hello.
- [x] Is is a mixture of two different things.
- [ ] It is a prize.

Find the word again in the extract and re-read the sentence around it. Choose the option that makes the most sense in context.

5 a How often do the bolving championships take place? Write your answer below.

once a year

The text doesn't state 'once a year'. You have to look for another word that tells you this ('annual').

b Which word tells you this? Find and copy it.

annual

Make sure you copy the word carefully.

Guided questions

This extract continues the 'Brilliant Bolving' article.

Bryony, a ranger for the Eastern Moors Project that organises the event in the Peak District, explains: 'Anyone can enter the competition, and we have a special category for junior entrants. Points are awarded for authenticity and volume, however the ultimate measure of success is to receive a reply from another deer. The championships provide a fun way for people to come along and learn about the red deer and their environment.'

Fun it most certainly seems to be! I arrive on Big Moor in the Peak District one early evening in autumn and am greeted by a group of people wrapped up in warm clothing, chatting and drinking hot chocolate. The excited bolving participants peer through binoculars in the hope of spotting the deer and clear their throats in preparation for their big moment on the moor. Then the contest begins.

1 Which type of text is this? Tick **one** box.

☐ fiction　　　　☐ instructional text

☐ informal newspaper report　　☐ scientific report

> Look at the use of an exclamation mark in the second paragraph. This sets a relaxed, conversational tone.

2 The first paragraph presents some text in speech marks. Why?

☐ because it is reported speech

☐ because it is direct speech

☐ because it is a quotation from a well-known figure

> Think about what makes these words different from the rest of the text.

3 a From your reading of the text, is the statement below true or false? Tick **one** box.

The most successful participants produce a quiet sound to call to the deer.

☐ true　　☐ false

b Which phrase tells you this? Find and copy it.

> Look for the section in the text that describes how points are awarded to the competitors.

4 a Why does the Eastern Moors Project organise bolving competitions? Tick **one** box.

☐ because they want to scare away the deer

☐ because they want the public to find out more about deer

☐ because they want more members of the public to see deer

☐ because they want to communicate with deer

b Which sentence tells you this? Find and copy it.

5 Find and copy a word that means 'best' or 'greatest'.

Have a go

This extract continues the 'Brilliant Bolving' article.

A hush descends on the crowd as the first contestant, Krish, slowly steps forward. Cupping his hands around his mouth to amplify the sound, he bellows out across the moorland. There's an expectant silence as everyone strains to hear if any deer respond to his call, but there's nothing this time. The judges are jotting notes on their clipboards.

The next contestant, Holly, steps forward. Holly looks about ten years of age. She takes a deep breath and, forming a mini loud speaker with her hands, bolvers at the top of her lungs. I am amazed at how someone so small could produce such a deep, booming sound! The deer are obviously impressed too – from somewhere on the other side of the moor a stag sends his thunderous reply.

1 mark

1 a In which tense is the text written? Write your answer below. •——

> Look at verbs to help you work out the tense.

_____

1 mark

2 Find and copy a word in the text that means 'to make a sound louder'.

_____

3 a Why does the writer start the first paragraph with a hush descending on the crowd?

- [ ] to make the atmosphere seem tense
- [ ] to show it is a dangerous competition
- [ ] because Krish is the main character

2 marks

b What does 'thunderous' mean? Tick **one** box.

- [ ] like a deer
- [ ] very loud
- [ ] very quiet
- [ ] strange sounding

1 mark

4 Find and copy a word in the text that means 'hopeful' or 'excited'. •——

> Your word should be the same part of speech as the ones in the question.

_____

Beyond the exam

Write your own article about an event or competition that you have attended. Your article needs to be interesting for your reader, so think carefully about:

- the structure of your writing
- your language choices.

Time to reflect

Mark your *Have a go* section out of 5. How are you doing so far?

Check your answers in the back of the book and write your score in the progress chart.

Had a go *0–2 marks*	**Nearly there** *3–4 marks*	**Nailed it!** *5 marks*
Have another look at the *Worked examples* on page 50. Then try these questions again.	Look at your incorrect answers. Make sure you understand how to get the correct answer.	Congratulations! Now see whether you can get full marks on the *Timed practice*.

When you are ready, try the *Timed practice* on the next page.

Timed practice

⏱ 15

This extract is from an information leaflet about wildlife in the UK.

Red deer

Red deer are the largest native land mammal in the UK. They are herbivores and eat mainly heather, grass and tree bark. They live together in herds. Their habitats are mainly remote moorlands – far from heavily-populated, urban areas – where the herds are able to roam freely. Their dark red coats camouflage them amongst the heather and bracken of moorlands, which enables them to hide easily. As bears and wolves are extinct in Britain, the deer here no longer have any natural predators. However, their young calves are vulnerable to attacks by eagles and foxes.

The red deer family

Male deer, known as stags, grow antlers. The age of a stag is estimated by the number of spikes on its antlers: the older it is, the more spikes it will have. A year-old male deer with its first set of short, unbranched antlers is called a 'pricket'. A 'hart' is the name for a stag over the age of five years, and a stag of fourteen or more is called an 'imperial'.

1 The word 'remote' can mean 'aloof and unfriendly', but in this text it has a different meaning. Explain in your own words what it means here.

_____

_____

> 1
> mark

2 a Is the clause below written in the active or passive voice? Write your answer below.

The age of a stag is estimated by the number of spikes on his antlers

_____

> 1
> mark

3 Which type of text feature is 'The red deer family'? Tick **one** box.

☐ quotation   ☐ illustration   ☐ bullet point   ☐ subheading

> 1
> mark

4 Find and copy a word that means a young stag with antlers that haven't yet branched.

_____

> 1
> mark

5 a From your reading of the text, is the statement below true or false? Tick **one** box.

Deer do not eat meat.

☐ true   ☐ false

b Which word tells you this? Find and copy it. _____

> 2
> marks

6 What does the word 'vulnerable' mean?

☐ susceptible   ☐ indestructible   ☐ frequently   ☐ helpless

> 1
> mark

Time to reflect

Mark your *Timed practice* section out of 7. How did you do?

Check your answers in the back of the book and write your score in the progress chart.

☐ *0–5 marks*
Scan the QR code for extra practice.
Then move on to the next practice section or
try Test 22 in your Ten-Minute Tests book.

☐ *6–7 marks*
Well done!
Move on to the next practice section or try Test 22
in your Ten-Minute Tests book.

11 Explaining texts

Writers choose their language and structure carefully to make the reader think and feel particular things. For some comprehension questions you may have to identify what choices the writer has made and explain what effect his has on the reader.

Worked examples

This non-fiction extract is from a newspaper article about the anniversary of an important milestone in the history of women's rights.

2 February 2018 marked the centenary of The Representation of the People Act. This was an act passed by Parliament granting women the right to vote in elections. It has only been in the last century that British women have been able to participate in politics.

Although the act heralded a new era in female empowerment, it only applied to women who were over the age of 30 and owned property. Younger and less affluent women remained disenfranchised until a decade later when all women over 21 were permitted to vote.

Emmeline Pankhurst

abc 'Disenfranchised' means 'not allowed to vote'.

None of these advancements in establishing equality for women would have happened without a long campaign fought by a group of women called the suffragettes and their leader Emmeline Pankhurst.

1 a Is the style of this text formal or informal? Write your answer below.

<u>   formal   </u>

> Look at the type of words used. Long, complex words suggest a formal style.

b Why do you think it is it written in this style? Tick **one** box.

- [ ] It is a set in the past.
- [x] It is a factual account.
- [ ] It is a fictitious story.
- [ ] It is a narrative.

> A formal style is usually used in a factual account to make the writer sound professional and knowledgeable. This encourages the reader to trust them.

2 Find and copy a verb in the text that means 'given permission'.

<u>   permitted   </u>

> The verb in the text uses the same root word (permit).

3 What does 'affluent' mean? Write your answer below.

<u>   wealthy   </u>

> If you don't know the word, read the sentence it is in and try to think of another word you could replace it with that would make sense.

4 a In February 2018 how many years had passed since women were given the right to vote? Write your answer below

<u>   100 years   </u>

b Find and copy a word that tells you this.

<u>   century   </u>

> The text doesn't state the number of years, so you have to look for other words that tell you this information ('centenary').

5 Explain in your own words why the writer has chosen to add a subheading to the last paragraph.

<u>to show the reader that they are moving on to a new topic</u>

> When answering a 'why' question, think about what the writer's choice makes the reader think or feel.

Guided questions

In this fiction text, the writer imagines what life was like for suffragette Emmeline Pankhurst's daughter, Christabel.

My name is Christabel Pankhurst. I am the eldest daughter of Emmeline and Dr Richard Pankhurst. I was born in Manchester, but we moved to London when I was young. My earliest childhood memories are of meetings held at our home in Russell Square, where women's rights activists would meet to plan their campaigns.

Most men of our time refused to learn about or even consider our movement. However, my late father was enlightened. He once said: 'If a body was half of it bound, how was it expected that it would grow and develop properly?'

People sometimes ask me if I would have become a suffragette if it weren't for mother. The answer is of course a resounding yes! I believe it is our duty as women to make this world a better place for ourselves and our children.

1 a Is this text written in the first or third person? Write your answer below. •——

> The first person uses 'I'. The third person uses 'he', 'she' or 'it'.

_____

b Why has the writer chosen this viewpoint? Tick **one** box. •——

> Try changing a few sentences from the first to the third person, and think about how it affects your thoughts and feelings.

☐ to create a feeling of mystery

☐ to help the reader understand Christabel's point of view

☐ to help the reader understand Dr Pankhurst's point of view

2 The second paragraph presents some text in speech marks. Explain why. •——

> Think about who said the words.

_____

_____

3 a From your reading of the text, is the statement below true or false? Tick **one** box. •——

> Look for the paragraph that includes the keyword 'father'.

Christabel's father was alive when she wrote this account.

☐ true

☐ false

b Which word tells you this? Find and copy it.

_____

4 What does 'enlightened' mean? Tick **one** box. •——

> Think about how Christabel compares her father to other men of the time.

☐ good at presenting his opinion

☐ has strong religious views

☐ a doctor of medicine

☐ has modern, well-informed opinions

5 Why is the last line an effective way for the writer to end this text? •——

> Think about how the focus changes in the last sentence.

It is effective because _____

_____

Have a go

This non-fiction text is an extract from a history book. It provides more information about the suffragette movement.

The leader of the suffragettes in the early twentieth century was a woman named Emmeline Pankhurst. She has gone down in history for her single-minded determination to secure the vote for women. In that era, women were regarded as second-class citizens and only men held positions of power. Pankhurst led protests and marches throughout the country to challenge this.

On some occasions, the suffragettes took dramatic, and occasionally aggressive, measures in order to bring attention to their cause. In 1908 two women chained themselves to railings outside the Prime Minister's house. They did this so that the politicians inside and the gathering crowd on the street would hear what had to say before the police could remove the chains and take them away.

In upholding their beliefs, the suffragettes often experienced great suffering. Many were imprisoned and treated harshly for their beliefs. However, they ultimately achieved their long fought-for goal of female emancipation.

1 a From your reading of the text, is the statement below true or false? Tick **one** box.

The suffragettes always used peaceful methods of protest.

☐ true ☐ false

2 marks

b Which word or phrase tells you this? _____

1 mark

2 Find and copy a phrase that means 'freedom and equality for women'. _____

3 Why is the last sentence an effective way to end the text? Tick **one** box.

> To answer questions that use the word 'effective', think about what feelings you had when you read the text.

☐ It tells you more about Emmeline Pankhurst.

☐ It makes the reader feel sorry for the suffragettes.

☐ It tells the reader what the suffragettes achieved in the end.

1 mark

☐ It inspires the reader to stand up for their beliefs.

1 mark

4 Find and copy a word in the text that means 'a period of time in history'. _____

5 Why does the writer explain in detail the story of the two suffragettes who chained themselves to railings?

> Think about what it is an example of and how it gives the reader more information.

_____

1 mark

_____

_____

Time to reflect

Mark your *Have a go* section out of 6. How are you doing so far?

Check your answers in the back of the book and see how you are doing.

☐ **Had a go**
0–3 marks

☐ **Nearly there**
4–5 marks

☐ **Nailed it!**
6 marks

Have another look at the *Worked examples* on page 54. Then try these questions again.

Look at your incorrect answers. Make sure you understand how to get the correct answer.

Congratulations! Now see whether you can get full marks on the *Timed practice*.

When you are ready, try the *Timed practice* on the next page.

Timed practice

15

In this fiction text, the writer imagines Christabel Pankhurst writing to Olivia Smith, a fellow suffragette who was imprisoned for chaining herself to railings outside the Prime Minister's house.

31 January 1908

Dear Olivia,

I hope this letter reaches you safely and that your spirits are bearing up during your incarceration. It was extremely brave of you and Miss New to chain yourself to the railings outside the Prime Minister's house. It is even more courageous, Mother and I both feel, for you to elect to spend three weeks in prison rather than pay the fine. As you know, I myself have spent time in prison and understand how you must be feeling. My dear Olivia, you are an example and inspiration to us all in our battle for equality.

Please take care of yourself as best you can. Three weeks must seem like an eternity in that dreadful place, but you will soon be free – free to take up the cause and fight again! Your sacrifice won't have been in vain.

Your loving friend,

Christabel

1 a Which type of text has the writer chosen to use? _____

   b What is the effect of this? Tick **one** box.

     ⬜ It provides a factual account in a formal style.

     ⬜ It helps bring the past to life for the reader.

     ⬜ It helps the reader to feel sorry for the Prime Minister.

2 What does 'incarceration' mean? Tick **one** box.

  ⬜ stay   ⬜ imprisonment   ⬜ jail   ⬜ protest

3 Find and copy a word that means 'to make a choice to do something'. _____

4 a Find a phrase at the end of the text that tells you Christabel believes that Olivia's sacrifice will make a difference.

_____

   b Why is this sentence placed at the end of the text?

     ⬜ to leave Olivia with a positive and motivational message

     ⬜ because Christabel forgot to write it at the start

     ⬜ because it gives Olivia an important instruction

2 marks

1 mark

1 mark

2 marks

Time to reflect

Mark your *Timed practice* section out of 6. How did you do?

Check your answers in the back of the book and write your score in the progress chart.

⬜ *0–4 marks*
Scan the QR code for extra practice.
Then move on to the next practice section or try Test 23 in your Ten-Minute Tests book.

⬜ *5–6 marks*
Well done!
Move on to the next practice section or try Test 23 in your Ten-Minute Tests book.

12 Giving your opinion

Comprehension questions may ask you give your own opinion about a situation or a character.

Worked examples

This text is from a short story called 'Fanny and Annie' by D. H. Lawrence. It is about a woman returning home to marry a man named Harry who she has known since she was young. In this extract she catches sight of him waiting for her as her train pulls into the station.

Flame lurid his face as he turned among the throng of flame-lit and dark faces upon the platform. In the light of the furnace she caught sighting of his drifting countenance, like a piece of floating fire. And the nostalgia, the doom of homecoming went through her veins like a drug. His eternal face, flame-lit now! The pulse and darkness of the red fire from the furnace towers in the sky, lightening the desultory, industrial crowd on the wayside station, lit him and went out.

Of course he did not see her. Flame-lit and unseeing! Always the same, with his meeting eyebrows, his common cap, and his red-and-black scarf knotted round his throat. Not even a collar to meet her! The flames had sunk, there was shadow.

1 a Find and copy a phrase that describes the woman's feelings about returning home.

the doom of homecoming

b Explain what this phrase tells you about how she feels.

She feels upset about coming back home.

2 a The writer says that Harry's face is 'like a piece of floating fire'. Which literary device is this? Write your answer below.

simile

b Why is this an effective image? Tick **one** box.

- [ ] because it shows that he looks out of control
- [ ] because it shows that he has red hair
- [x] because it shows how striking his face is when lit up

3 a How does the woman feel about the way Harry is dressed? Tick **one** box.

- [ ] She is pleased.
- [x] She is disappointed that he isn't smarter.
- [ ] She does not care.

b Which words tell the reader this?

his common cap, and his red-and-black scarf knotted round his throat. Not even a collar to meet her!

4 Do you think she is right to feel this?

Yes, I think she is right to feel disappointed because it is an important occasion and he should dress in the right way.

abc
- 'Desultory' means 'lacking in purpose'
- Furnace towers are enormous factory chimneys
- 'Countenance' means 'face'
- 'Nostalgia' means 'wistful longing for the past'.

The writer makes a direct comparison between two things, using the word 'like'.

Use your answers to the earlier questions and clues from the text to help you form an opinion.

There is no right or wrong answer to this question but try to follow these steps:

1 state your opinion clearly
2 explain why you think that.

You don't have to agree, as long as you give a good reason for your opinion.

Guided questions

This text continues the story by D. H. Lawrence.

She opened the door of her grimy, branch-line carriage, and began to get down her bags. The porter was nowhere of course, but there was Harry, obscure, on the outer edge of the little crowd, missing her of course.

Her soul groaned within her, as he clambered into the carriage after her bags. Up shot the fire in the twilight sky, from the great furnace behind the station. She felt the red flame go across her face. She had come back, she had come back for good. And her spirit groaned dismally. She doubted if she could bear it.

There on the sordid little station under the furnaces, she stood, tall and distinguished in her well-made coat and skirt and her broad grey velour hat. She held her umbrella, her bead chatelaine, and a little leather case in her grey-gloved hands, while Harry staggered out of the ugly little train with her bags.

'There's a trunk at the back,' she said in her bright voice. But she was not feeling bright.

1 Why did the woman start getting her bags down on her own? Tick **one** box.

☐ because the train had arrived early

☐ because she couldn't find the porter

☐ because Harry didn't want to do it

> Look closely in the text for the keyword 'bags'.

> **abc**
> - 'Obscure' means 'difficult to see or understand'.
> - A 'bead chatelaine' is a small, decorative bag.

2 Explain why the phrase 'her spirit groaned' effectively shows how the woman feels about coming home.

> Think about why and when people groan.

_____

_____

3 Find and copy one adjective that tells the reader that the train station was dirty.

> Remember that adjectives usually come before the noun they describe.

_____

4 The writer describes the woman as standing 'tall and distinguished in her well-made coat and skirt and her broad grey velour hat'. What impression does this create of her? Tick **one** box.

☐ The woman is wearing warm clothing because it is cold.

☐ The woman is very important and has come to inspect the station.

☐ The woman is quite wealthy and looks out of place in the dirty railway station.

> Think about which type of person might wear those types of clothes.

5 Which words tell the reader that the woman is trying to hide her true feelings? Find and copy them.

> Look at how she speaks to Harry.

_____

6 Do you feel sorry for Harry? Explain why.

> Begin you answer with one of these options:
> - I feel sorry for Harry because…
> - I don't feel sorry for Harry because…

_____

_____

_____

_____

Have a go

This text is from a short story about a girl called Parveen who is playing in an important football match.

Suddenly, the world receded and time seemed to expand. The roar and cry of the crowd spiralled away, like water down a plughole. All that was left was Parveen, the ball and the goal. She drank down several slow, deep breaths, patiently calming her thumping heart, before setting her sights on her target. The goal grinned foolishly wide, almost inviting the perfect strike.

A fierce joy rushed through her veins. She began a graceful swing for the kick, when the cruel voice from the changing rooms tore through her mind. 'Beat us and you're dead, loser.'

1 The writer describes the sound of Parveen's heart as 'thumping'. Which literary device is this? Write your answer below.

_____

1 mark

2 The writer describes how the goal 'grinned foolishly wide, almost inviting the perfect strike'.

> Think about the human qualities the goal is given.

  a Which literary device is used? _____

  b What does the description show about Parveen's confidence in scoring a goal?

☐ She was confident.   ☐ She was not very confident.   ☐ She was worried she would miss.

2 marks

3 What does the phrase 'time seemed to expand' mean? Tick **one** box.

☐ There is only a few seconds left of the match.

☐ Time is moving very quickly because the match is so exciting.

☐ Parveen feels as though she is moving in slow motion.

1 mark

> Remember to state your opinion and then explain it by referring to the text.

4 Do you think that Parveen should try her best to score the goal?

_____

_____

_____

_____

2 marks

Time to reflect

Mark your *Have a go* section out of 6. How are you doing so far?

Check your answers in the back of the book and see how you are doing.

☐ **Had a go**
0–3 marks

☐ **Nearly there**
4–5 marks

☐ **Nailed it!**
6 marks

Have another look at the *Worked examples* on page 58. Then try these questions again.

Look at your incorrect answers. Make sure you understand how to get the correct answer.

Congratulations! Now see whether you can get full marks on the *Timed practice*.

When you are ready, try the *Timed practice* on the next page.

This text is from a story about a boy called Jacob and his little brother Ted going to school on a snowy day.

At break, Jacob raced into the cloakroom to put on his brand new wellies. Just as he was about to launch himself out into the playground, his ears caught a damp sniffling and snuffling from the corner. A forlorn figure was hunched under the hanging coats like an abandoned schoolbag.

A bolt of anger flashed through Jacob. The figure was his little brother Ted, his shoulders heaving with sobs.

'Ted! What's the matter? Has someone been mean to you?'

'Miss Li says I can't go outside to play… I forgot my wellies…' Ted spluttered.

Through the window, Jacob glimpsed the opening shots of the snowball fight soaring through the air. He hesitated. He should be out there right now, leading his brave troops into battle against the dastardly Year 6.

His eyes flooding with misery, Ted clumsily reached out a cold, sticky hand for Jacob's, just like he used to do when he was little. Jacob sighed. With a heavy heart, he pulled off his wellies and handed them to Ted.

'Here, take mine. I'm going to board game club anyway. If we get some extra socks from the lost property box they'll just about fit.'

1 Find and copy a phrase that shows how excited Jacob is about the snowball fight.

_____

1 mark

2 a Find and copy a metaphor that tells the reader that Ted thinks the snowball fight will be dramatic.

_____

b Explain the effect this metaphor has on the reader.

_____

2 marks

3 'With a heavy heart, he pulled off his wellies and handed them to Ted.'

This sentence tells the reader that Jacob feels sad about handing over his wellies. What else does it tell us about him? Tick **one** box.

☐ He is generous. ☐ He likes board game club more than the snow.

☐ He shouldn't give his boots to Ted. ☐ He is selfish.

1 mark

4 Explain in your own words which type of person you think Jacob is and why you believe this.

_____
_____
_____

2 marks

Time to reflect

Mark your *Timed practice* section out of 6. How did you do?
Check your answers in the back of the book and write your score in the progress chart.

☐ *0–4 marks*
Scan the QR code for extra practice.
Then move on to the next practice section or try Test 24 in your Ten-Minute Tests book.

☐ *5–6 marks*
Well done!
Move on to the next practice section or try Test 24 in your Ten-Minute Tests book.

13 Explaining poetry

Writers often use language techniques in their poetry to shape what the reader thinks and feels. In your 11+ test, you may be asked to explain the language in a poem and give your own response to it.

Worked examples

This is the first verse of the poem 'Winter' by Robert Louis Stevenson.

In rigorous hours, when down the iron lane

The redbreast looks in vain

For hips or haws,

Lo, shining flowers upon my window pane

The silver pencil of the winter draws.

abc
- 'Hips' are berries from a rose plant.
- 'Haws' are berries from a hawthorn plant.

1 In this poem, the word 'rigorous' means 'tough' or 'hard'. Explain why the writer uses it here.

Look at the word in context by looking at the next line in the poem.

because winter is a difficult time for birds because they can't find food

2 a Which phrase tells you that the ground was frozen solid? Write your answer below.

the iron lane

The noun 'iron' is used as an adjective here.

b Which literary device is this? Tick **one** box.

☐ simile   ☐ personification   ☐ alliteration   ☑ metaphor

3 a Find and copy an example of alliteration in the poem.

hips or haws

abc Alliteration is a sequence of words that start with the same sound. The words must be next to each other or close together.

b Explain what the effect of this is.

It creates a rhythm that gives a sense of the robin hopping around looking for food.

4 a How do you think the writer feels about the frost on his window? Tick **one** box.

☐ annoyed because it is ugly   ☑ happy because it is beautiful   ☐ sad because it is harsh and rigorous.

b Which line tells you this? Find and copy it.

Lo, shining flowers upon my window pane

6 'The silver pen of winter draws'. Which literary device is this? Write your answer below.

personification

abc Personification is when a non-human thing is given human traits. For example, 'the sun smiled at us'.

7 Write two contrasting adjectives that describe the writer's view of winter.

1   *harsh*

2   *beautiful*

These two adjectives capture the contrasting responses expressed by the writer.

Guided questions

This is the second verse of the poem 'Winter' by Robert Louis Stevenson.

> When all the snowy hill
>
> And the bare woods are still;
>
> When snipes are silent in the frozen bogs,
>
> And all the garden garth is whelmed in mire,
>
> Lo, by the hearth, the laughter of the logs –
>
> More fair than roses, lo, the flowers of fire!

abc
- A 'snipe' is a bird that lives in marshes.
- 'Garth' is an old-fashioned word for a garden.

1 a Which phrase tells you that the fireside is a cheerful place to be in winter? Find and copy it.

> Look at the sound the log fire makes.

_____

b Which literary device is this? Tick **one** box.

☐ onomatopoeia ☐ metaphor ☐ personification ☐ simile

2 a Which line tells you that the fire is beautiful? Find and copy it.

_____

_____

b Which literary device is this? Write your answer below.

_____

3 a Find and copy a phrase that tells you the birds have stopped singing.

> Look for the lines that mention birds.

_____

b Which literary device is this?

_____

4 The first part of this verse uses the words 'snowy',' still', 'silent' and 'frozen'. The second part uses the words 'laughter', 'fair', 'roses' and 'fire'. What is the effect of these different word choices? Tick **one** box.

☐ It creates a sense of sadness in the second part.

☐ It creates a contrast between the first part and the second part.

☐ It creates a sense of warmth and cheerfulness in the first part.

☐ It creates a sense of misery in the whole poem.

> This is an opinion question. There is no right or wrong answer, but you must state your opinion clearly and give reasons to explain it using clues from the text.

5 Explain what this verse makes you feel about winter and why.

_____

_____

_____

Have a go

'The Eagle' by Alfred Lord Tennyson.

> He clasps the crag with crooked hands;
>
> Close to the sun in lonely lands,
>
> Ring'd with the azure world, he stands.
>
> The wrinkled sea beneath him crawls;
>
> He watches from his mountain walls,
>
> And like a thunderbolt he falls.

abc 'Azure' is a shade of blue.

The apostrophe in 'ring'd' shows that the letter 'e' has been missed out. It is an old fashioned way of writing 'ringed'.

1 What does the writer mean by 'ring'd with the azure world'? Tick **one** box.

1 mark

☐ The eagle is surrounded by sea.

☐ The eagle is surrounded by sky.

☐ The eagle has rings on his claws.

☐ The eagle's feathers are blue.

2 a Which phrase tells you that the eagle swoops down from the cliff? Find and copy it.

2 marks

_____

b Which literary device is this? _____

3 a 'The wrinkled sea beneath him crawls.' Which literary device is this? _____

b Explain in your own words what this makes you think or feel about the sea.

2 marks

_____

_____

4 How do you think the writer feels about the eagle? Select **one**.

1 mark

☐ He is afraid of it.

☐ He thinks the eagle is an ugly creature.

☐ He feels a sense of awe and admiration.

Beyond the exam

Write a short poem about your favourite animal. Show how you feel about this animal by using literary devices.

Time to reflect

Mark your *Have a go* section out of 6. How are you doing so far?

Check your answers in the back of the book and see how you are doing.

☐ **Had a go** *0–4 marks*	☐ **Nearly there** *4–5 marks*	☐ **Nailed it!** *6 marks*
Have another look at the *Worked examples* on page 62. Then try these questions again.	Look at your incorrect answers. Make sure you understand how to get the correct answer.	Congratulations! Now see whether you can get full marks on the *Timed practice*.

When you are ready, try the *Timed practice* on the next page.

Timed practice

15

'Hope Is the Thing with Feathers' by Emily Dickinson

1 Hope is the thing with feathers
That perches in the soul,
And sings the tune without the words,
And never stops at all,

2 And sweetest in the gale is heard;
And sore must be the storm
That could abash the little bird
That kept so many warm.

3 I've heard it in the chilliest land,
And on the strangest sea;
Yet, never, in extremity,
It asked a crumb of me.

1 a What emotion is symbolised by the bird in this poem? Write your answer below.

_____

b Which literary device is used to show this? Tick **one** box.

☐ simile   ☐ onomatopoeia   ☐ alliteration   ☐ metaphor

2 marks

2 a Which literary device is the phrase 'strangest sea' an example of? Tick **one** box.

☐ simile   ☐ alliteration   ☐ personification   ☐ onomatopoeia

b What effect might the writer have wanted to create with this phrase? Tick **one** box.

☐ to show that the bird is in danger

☐ to recreate the sound of the sea

2 marks

3 What does the writer mean by the words 'That kept so many warm'? Tick **one** box.

☐ Some people can find hope and comfort by going to sea.

☐ Hope has given comfort to many people in difficult times.

☐ Birds' feathers are used in bedding to keep people warm.

☐ It is cold at sea so you must wear warm clothing.

1 mark

4 Do you think the writer has ever lost hope? Explain why you think this.

_____

_____

_____

2 marks

Time to reflect

Mark your _Timed practice_ section out of 7. How did you do?
Check your answers in the back of the book and write your score in the progress chart.

☐ **0–5 marks**
Scan the QR code for extra practice.
Then move on to the next practice section or try Test 25 in your Ten-Minute Tests book.

☐ **6–7 marks**
Well done!
Move on to the next practice section or try Test 25 in your Ten-Minute Tests book.

Checkpoint 3

In this checkpoint you will practise skills from the **Comprehension** topic. There are four short texts followed by questions for you to answer.

This is an extract from the poem 'Daffodils' by William Wordsworth.

30

1 I wander'd lonely as a cloud

That floats on high o'ver vales and hills,

When all at once I saw a crowd,

A host, of golden daffodils;

Beside the lake, beneath the trees,

Fluttering and dancing in the breeze.

2 Continuous as the stars that shine

And twinkle on the Milky Way,

They stretch'd in never-ending line

Along the margins of a bay:

Ten thousand saw I at a glance,

Tossing their heads in sprightly dance.

1 a The writer describes the daffodils as 'dancing in the breeze'. Which literary device is this? ← Section 13

☐ metaphor ☐ simile ☐ personification

b Find and copy another example of this device.

_____

2 marks

2 'I wander'd lonely as a cloud'. What does this line tell you about how the writer feels? Tick **one** box. ← Section 13

☐ He feels lost.
☐ He feels carefree.
☐ He feels dizzy.
☐ He feels sad.

1 mark

3 The writer compares the daffodils to stars in the Milky Way. Which literary device is this? Tick **one** box. ← Section 13

☐ metaphor ☐ alliteration ☐ simile ☐ personification

1 mark

4 Find and copy a word from the second stanza that means 'edge' or 'border'. ← Section 13

_____

1 mark

5 How do you think the writer of this poem feels? Explain your answer. ← Section 13

_____

_____

_____

2 marks

This fiction extract is from 'Dracula' by Bram Stoker. In this section, the narrator describes his first meeting with the Count.

Hitherto I had noticed the backs of his hands as they lay on his knees in the firelight, and they had seemed rather white and fine, but seeing them close to me, I could only notice that they were rather course – broad with squat fingers. Strange to say, there were hairs in the centre of the palm. The nails were long and fine, and cut to a sharp point. As the Count leaned over me and his hands touched me, I could not repress a shudder. It may have been that his breath was rank, but a horrible feeling of nausea came over me, which, do what I would, I could not conceal.

The Count, evidently noticing it, drew back. And with a grim sort of smile, which showed more than he had yet done his protuberant teeth, sat himself down again on his own side of the fireplace. We were both silent for a while, and as I looked towards the window I saw the first dim streak of the coming dawn. There seemed a strange stillness over everything. But as I listened, I heard as if from down below in the valley the howling of many wolves. The Count's eyes gleamed and he said:

'Listen to them – the children of the night. What music they make!'

6 a Explain what is strange about the Count's hands.   Section 10

_____

_____

   b What effect does this have? Tick **one** box.

    ☐ It makes the Count's hands seem delicate and gentle.

    ☐ It makes the Count's hands seem like an animal's paws.

    ☐ It makes the Count's finger nails seem dirty.

    ☐ It makes the reader like him.

2 marks

7 a Explain how the narrator feels when the Count touches him.   Section 10

_____

_____

   b The Count gives a 'grim sort of smile'. Why do you think he responds like this? Tick **one** box.

    ☐ He is upset because the narrator is being rude to him.

    ☐ He doesn't understand why the narrator's reaction.

    ☐ He is secretly pleased by the narrator's reaction.

2 marks

8 Find and copy a word that means 'sticking out'.   Section 10

1 mark

_____

9 a What does the Count compare the sound of the wolves to? Write your answer below.   Section 10

_____

   b Explain how this sound helps create a frightening atmosphere.

_____

_____

_____

2 marks

This extract is from a speech in the play 'As you Like It' by William Shakespeare.

> All the world's a stage
>
> And all the men and women merely players
>
> They have their exits and entrances
>
> And one man in his time plays many parts,
>
> His acts being seven ages. At first the infant,
>
> Mewling and puking in the nurse's arms,
>
> And then the whining schoolboy, with his satchel,
>
> And shining morning face, creeping like a snail
>
> Unwillingly to school.

1 mark

10 The writer compares life to a play. Which literary device is this? Write your answer below.   ← Section 13

_____

11 a Which phrase describes the different stages in life?   ← Section 13

☐ His acts being seven ages   ☐ plays many parts   ☐ the world's a stage

b Explain whether you think this is an effective comparison.

2 marks

_____

_____

12 What does the line 'They have their exits and entrances' mean? Tick **one** box.   ← Section 13

☐ Everyone gets to know different people in their life.

1 mark

☐ Actors and actresses like to dress up for different parts.

☐ Everybody is born and dies.

13 Do you think the writer likes babies? Explain your opinion.   ← Section 13

2 marks

_____

_____

1 mark

14 Find and copy a word that means 'complaining in an irritating way'.   ← Section 13

_____

15 a The writer describes the schoolboy as 'creeping like a snail unwillingly to school'. Which literary device is this?   ← Section 13

_____

b What does this tell you? Tick **one** box.

☐ His face shines like a snail's shell.

2 marks

☐ He walks very slowly because he doesn't want to go to school.

☐ He has a heavy bag to carry.

This extract is from a sports magazine and is an advert for trainers .

Cheetah Sneakers

Are your old trainers letting you down?

You need to fling the spring back into your step by investing in a pair of Cheetah Sneakers! They have all these great features:

- high visibility for late night jogging
- low-cut design for freedom of movement
- choice of three stylish colours.
- durable insole support
- cushioned ankle area

Cheetah Sneakers give you purringly perfect performance for just £56.00. Hurry while stocks last!

16 What is the aim of this text? Select **one**.

☐   to describe the habits of cheetahs

☐   to persuade people to buy a brand of trainers

☐   to provide a technical description of different types of trainers

☐   to provide information on staying safe when jogging

Section 10

1 mark

17 Why are the words 'Cheetah Sneakers' repeated three times? Write your answer below.

Section 11

1 mark

_____

18 Which word means 'hardwearing' or 'long-lasting'.

☐ investing   ☐ visibility   ☐ durable   ☐ stylish

Section 10

1 mark

19 The trainers provide 'a purringly perfect performance'. Which literary device is this?

Section 10

1 mark

_____

20 Find and copy a word that means 'buying': _____

Section 10

1 mark

21 Why does the writer use the phrase 'Hurry while stocks last!'?

☐   because they don't have much patience

☐   to show the reader that they want the shoes too

☐   to persuade readers to buy the shoes quickly

Section 11

1 mark

22 Do you think it is right to spend so much on a pair of shoes? Explain why you think this.

Section 12

2 marks

_____

_____

Mark your *Checkpoint* out of 31. How did you do?

1 Check your answers in the back of the book and write your score in the progress chart. If any of your answers are incorrect, use the section links to find out which practice sections to look at again.

2 Scan the QR code for extra practice.

3 Move on to the next practice section.

14 Writing non-fiction

In the 11+ test you might be asked to write a non-fiction text. To do this successfully you will need to choose your text type, structure and language carefully. Essays, letters, articles and speeches are examples of non-fiction text types.

Worked example

1   Plan an essay using one of the titles below.

    a <u>My favourite hobby</u>

    b A memorable day

> You may be given a choice of titles. Choose the one you feel most comfortable with.

Competitions

How I got involved

My favourite hobby

Getting started

Why others should do it

Benefits

> Spend a few minutes gathering your ideas before you start writing

- Introduction: Grab the reader's interest. Introduce gymnastics.
- Middle: My experience – getting started, competitions and benefits.
- Conclusion: Reasons to try it. Encourage the reader.

> Writing a short plan is a good way to get your ideas in order. A piece of non-fiction should be structured in this way:
> - an **introduction** that provides an outline
> - a **middle** with two or three main points
> - a **conclusion** that summarises the main points and leaves a strong message.

Guided question

1   **a**   Complete the mind map below.

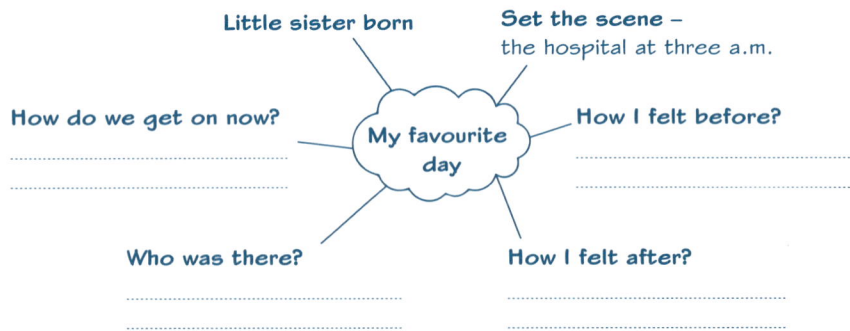

Little sister born

Set the scene – the hospital at three a.m.

How do we get on now?

My favourite day

How I felt before?

....

....

....

....

Who was there?

How I felt after?

....

....

....

....

    b   Put the plan below in order by writing 'introduction', 'middle' or 'conclusion' after the correct section.

- Reflect on how I feel about it now.   _____

- Describe what happened and how it felt.   _____

- Set the scene and explain who was there. _____

Beyond the exam

Write a letter to your local sports centre persuading them to set up a gymnastics club. You should include these features:
- a greeting ('Dear' and a name)
- a sign off ('Yours sincerely' and your name at the end).

Worked example

1 Write an essay using one of the titles below.

a My favourite hobby

b A memorable day

> My favourite hobby is gymnastics. I eat, sleep and breathe it! I first became interested when I saw gymnasts practising in my local sports centre. I was intrigued by their magical movements, so when I got home I tried to copy them. I was terrible at first, but when I started classes I soon got much better.
>
> About a year after I started lessons, I went to my first gymnastics competition. I was very nervous, but when I started my routine I found I loved performing for the judges. I even won a bronze medal! Since then, I've been to competitions all over the country, for example in Edinburgh, Liverpool, Manchester and London.
>
> However, gymnastics is not all about winning competitions. It is very good exercise, and learning the routines is a workout for your brain too! When I started I could only just do a forward roll, but now I can do somersaults, cartwheels and the splits! It is very satisfying to feel myself getting better and better.
>
> Starting gymnastics is the best thing I ever did. I would definitely recommend it to anyone looking for a fun, friendly and exciting sport!

These opening sentences introduce the topic and grab the reader's attention.

Use sophisticated language such as 'intrigued' to create a formal tone.

You can use interesting language features like alliteration.

Use conjunctions to link your ideas and structure your writing.

Give examples or stories from your personal experience.

Use features like lists to make your writing interesting for the reader.

Remember to start a new paragraph each time you start talking about a new subject.

If possible, use some technical language to show that you know your topic well.

End your essay with a conclusion that summarises your ideas.

Guided question

1 Use your imagination to fill in the gaps in the text below.

My favourite hobby is rugby. I _____ it because _____.

When I first started playing I was _____. For example, I _____. Luckily my coach is really

supportive and helped me improve. Now I _____

_____.

Beyond the exam

Ask an adult to recommend a newspaper article for you to read. Make a list of the features that are used in it. You could look for these things:

- subheadings
- formal language
- facts and numbers.

Guided question

1 Complete the paragraphs below from an essay with the title of 'My Favourite Place'.

I am lucky that there are many beautiful and interesting places close to my town. Only ten miles away you can find wide, stony beaches with cosy little cafes. In the centre of town, there is a busy main street with a library, shops and a cinema.

But the place which I love more than anywhere is ●—————

_____

There are lots of reasons why I love it so much. Firstly, _____

_____

_____

_____

_____

_____

When I am older I would like to travel and visit lots of places, but this

place will always be the most special to me because _____

_____

_____

> Continue the introduction by writing a short description of a place you love.

> Use adjectives and the senses to help your reader imagine being there.

> Complete the main part of the essay by explaining why you particularly like this place. You might choose to talk about a memory you have of that place, what you can do there or how it makes you feel.

> In the conclusion you should sum up why the place is special to you.

Have a go

1 Write an essay using one of the titles below. ●—————

  a My favourite holiday

  b My first year at school

  c My best friend

> Use the space below to plan your essay. You will need to write it on a separate piece of paper.

> • Plan the structure of your essay to make sure it contains an introduction, middle and conclusion.
> • Use formal language such as sophisticated words and long sentences.
> • Use correct punctuation and grammar.
> • Use non-fiction features, for example subheadings, lists and facts and figures.
> • Structure your text using paragraphs.

Beyond the exam

Choose a topic you are interested in and research three facts about it that you could include in an essay about that topic.

Timed practice

A good piece of non-fiction writing should include:

- a clear introduction explaining what the topic is
- a middle with two or three main points
- a conclusion that summarises your ideas
- formal language
- a range of correct punctuation
- non-fiction features, for example subheadings, lists and facts and figures.

This page gives you a selection of questions that you can use to practise writing non-fiction. Use the checklist to focus your writing.

Use a separate sheet of paper to plan and write your answer.

1 Write an essay with the title 'My neighbourhood'.

2 Complete the essay below.

Lots of people like cats or dogs, but my favourite animal is the penguin.

3 Write a letter to your headteacher asking permission to hold a charity cake sale at your school.

4 Write a speech about your favourite book.

5 Imagine that you run a charity that looks after abandoned animals. Write a letter to a newspaper persuading people to donate pet food.

6 Write a newspaper article about your school sports day.

7 Write an account of a memorable day in your life.

8 Write an essay about how to use the internet safely.

9 Write an essay with the title 'My perfect pet'.

Beyond the exam

Ask an adult to lend you a newspaper or magazine. Find as many advertisements as you can and write a list of any interesting words and phrases they use to grab the reader's attention. You could look for these features:

- headings and subheadings
- alliteration
- lists
- interesting language choices.

Progress test

Complete this test once you have worked through all the practice sections in this book. It covers all the topics in this book and is as hard as a real 11+ test.

Comprehension

(60)

Tropical Rainforests

Tropical rainforests are dense areas of jungle covering approximately 7 per cent of the Earth's surface. The main areas of tropical rainforest are located in South and Central America, West Africa and Indonesia. All these areas are situated around the Equator and have very warm and wet climates. The high precipitation (some rainforests can recieve up to 300 mm of rain per month), combined with average temperatures of around 28 °C, provides ideal conditions for an abundance of animals, insects and plants to thrive. Rainforests also produce 20 per cent of the world's oxygen, which is vital for our survival.

The largest tropical rainforest in the world is Amazonia in South America. This vast area of dense jungle is criss-crossed by thousands of rivers and their tributaries, including the second longest river in the world – the Amazon. Amazonia covers an enormous area that could swallow Great Britain around 24 times over. It includes most of north-western Brazil and spans six other countries. Amazonia has extraordinary biodiversity and it is estimated that it is home to 2.5 million species of insects, 1500 types of birds, over 2000 fish species and 4000 varieties of plants.

Tropical rainforests are often referred to as 'the world's largest pharmacy'. This is because a quarter of all natural medicines have been discovered in the plants that grow there, and there may still be many more for scientists to find. In addition to medicines, rubber, chocolate, bamboo, nuts and vanilla are all produced by rainforest plants.

In light of all these benefits, you would think that mankind would fiercely protect the rainforests. Sadly, though, this is not the case. Rainforests are rapidly shrinking as large areas are cut down to clear space for logging, farming, mining and building.

So why is this destruction permitted? The governments of many poorer countries feel that they have no choice, as the resources and land in the rainforest are an importance source of income and jobs for ever-growing populations. In order to protect what is left of the rainforest, we must find a way to support and develop these countries so that they can use their resources in a more sustainable way. A balance must be found between the needs of nature and the needs of humankind.

1 Find and copy a word that means 'the variety of animal and plant life in an area'.

Section 10

1 mark

_____

2 What does 'precipitation' mean? Tick **one** box.

Section 10

- [ ] high temperatures
- [ ] rain, snow, sleet or hail
- [ ] sweating to lower body temperature
- [ ] strong winds

1 mark

3 Is the statement below true or false? Tick **one** box. Section 10

Tropical rainforests are situated on or near the Equator.

☐ true

☐ false

1 mark

4 What is the main theme of the third paragraph? Tick **one** box. Section 11

☐ the different species of animals in the rainforest

☐ the resources we get from the rainforest

☐ the tribes of people who live in the rainforest

☐ the destruction of the rainforest

1 mark

5 Which phrase is often used to describe the large amount of medicine found in the rainforests? Find and copy it. Section 10

_____

1 mark

6 Write two products that come from the rainforest. Section 10

1 _____

2 _____

2 marks

7 a Why do governments allow large areas of the rainforest to be cut down? Write your answer below. Section 11

_____

_____

_____

1 mark

b Do you believe that they should be allowed to do so? Explain your opinion. Section 12

_____

_____

_____

_____

2 marks

The following extract is from a short story by Katherine Mansfield called 'The Voyage'. In this section, a girl named Fenella and her grandmother are setting sail on a boat.

The Picton boat was due to leave at half past eleven. It was a beautiful night, mild, starry, only when they got out of the cab and started to walk down the Old Wharf that jutted out into the harbour, a faint wind blowing off the water ruffled under Fenella's hat, and she put up her hand to keep it on. It was dark on the Old Wharf, very dark, the wool sheds, the cattle trucks, the cranes standing up so high, the little squat railway engine, all seemed carved out of solid darkness. Here and there on a rounded wood-pile, that was like a stalk of a huge black mushroom, there hung a lantern, but it seemed afraid to unfurl its timid quivering light in all that blackness; it burned softly, as if for itself.

Then suddenly, so suddenly that Fenella and her grandma both leapt, there sounded from behind the largest wool shed, that had a trial of smoke hanging over it, *Mia-oo-oo-O-O!*

'First whistle,' said her father briefly, and in that moment they came in sight of the Picton boat. Lying beside the dark wharf, all strung, all beaded with round golden lights, the Picton boat looked as if she was more ready to sail among stars than out into the cold sea. People pressed along the gangway. First went her grandma, then her father, then Fenella. There was a high step down on to the deck, and an old sailor in a jersey standing by gave her his dry, hard hand. They were there; they stepped out of the way of the hurrying people and standing under a little iron stairway that led to the upper deck they began to say good-bye.

'There mother, there's your luggage!' said Fenella's father, giving Grandma another strapped-up sausage.

'Thank you, Frank.'

'And you've got your cabin tickets safe?'

'Yes, dear.'

'And your other tickets?'

Grandma felt for them inside her glove and showed him the tips.

'That's right.'

He sounded stern, but Fenella, eagerly watching him, saw that he looked tired and sad. *Mia-oo-oo-O-O!* The second whistle blared just above their heads, and a voice like a cry shouted, 'Any more for the gangway?'

'You'll give my love to Father,' Fenella saw her father's lips say. And her grandma, very agitated, answered, 'Of course I will dear. Go now. You'll be left. Go now, Frank.'

As the boat arrives in Picton Fenella and her grandma go out on deck

But if it had been cold in the cabin, on deck it was like ice. The sun was not up yet, but the stars were dim, and the cold pale sky was the same colour as the cold pale sea. On the land a white mist rose and fell. Now they could see quite plainly dark bush. Even the shapes of the umbrella ferns showed, and those strange silvery withered trees that are little skeletons … Now they could see the landing-stage and some little houses, pale too, clustered together, like shells on the lid of a box. The other passengers tramped up and down, but more slowly than they had the night before, and they looked gloomy.

And now the landing stage came out to meet them. Slowly it swam towards the Picton boat, and a man holding a coil of rope, and a cart with a small drooping horse and another man sitting on the step, came too.

'It's Mr Penreddy, Fenella, come for us,' said Grandma. She sounded pleased. Her white waxen cheeks were blue with cold, her chin trembled, and she had to keep wiping her eyes and her little pink nose.

8 What is the main theme of the first paragraph? Tick **one** box.   ⬅ Section 11

☐ Fenella's feelings

☐ the harbour

☐ the Picton boat

☐ the night sky

9 a The lantern 'seemed afraid to unfurl its timid quivering light in all that blackness'.
What does this tell you about the light? Write your answer below.

Section 13

_____

_____

b Which literary device is this? Write your answer below.

2 marks

_____

10 Find and copy a word that means 'short and wide'.

Section 11

1 mark

_____

11 Which phrase describes how it is hard to see the buildings and vehicles clearly? Find and copy it.

Section 11

1 mark

_____

12 Fenella's father gave Grandma 'another strapped-up sausage'. What does this tell you? Tick **one** box.

Section 11

☐ Grandma was greedy.

☐ Grandma was making hot dogs for the journey.

☐ Grandma's bag was full of sausages.

☐ The bags were wrapped up in sausage shapes.

1 mark

13 a The houses at Picton harbour are 'clustered together, like shells on the lid of a box'. Which literary device is this? Write your answer below.

Section 13

_____

b Explain in your own words why this description effective.

_____

_____

2 marks

14 a What did Fenella imagine the landing stage doing as the boat approached Picton harbour? Write your answer below.

Section 11

_____

_____

_____

b Which literary device is this? Write your answer below.

2 marks

_____

2 marks

15 In your opinion which type of person is Grandma? Explain your ideas.

Section 12

_____

_____

_____

_____

2 marks

Spelling, punctuation and grammar

16 Which sentence below is punctuated correctly? Tick **one** box.

Section 4

- ☐ 'When will we meet our new neighbours' asked Shelly.
- ☐ When will we meet our new neighbours' asked Shelly.
- ☐ 'When will we meet our new neighbours? asked Shelly.
- ☐ 'When will we meet our new neighbours?' asked Shelly.

1 mark

17 In which section is the punctuation mistake? Circle the correct number.

Section 4

'My mum lost her / purse last week,' said / Olivia, Fortunately someone / handed it in to the police.'

　　　　1　　　　　　　　2　　　　　　　　　　3　　　　　　　　　4

1 mark

18 Complete the sentence below by adding and correctly punctuating a parenthesis explaining the name of your school.

Our school _____ has six classes in each year group.

1 mark

19 Which sentence below is punctuated correctly? Tick **one** box.

Section 6

- ☐ Grandpas tools are locked in the shed.
- ☐ Grandpa's tools are locked in the shed.
- ☐ Grandpas' tools are locked in the shed.
- ☐ Grandpas tool's are locked in the shed.

1 mark

20 a Underline the conjunction in the sentence below.

Section 3

My aunt loves the coast but my uncle prefers the mountains.

b Which type of conjunction is it? Tick **one** box.

- ☐ subordinating
- ☐ coordinating

2 marks

21 Punctuate the sentence below using a possessive apostrophe.

Section 6

The womens toilets are on the right.

1 mark

22 Punctate the sentence below using a colon.

Section 5

The former American President Theodore Roosevelt said 'It's hard to fail, but it is worse never to have tried to succeed.'

1 mark

23 Which word below is spelled correctly? Tick **one** box.

Section 9

- ☐ parlliamnet
- ☐ parrliment
- ☐ parliament
- ☐ parlment

1 mark

24 a Which conjunction completes the sentence below? Tick **one** box. ⬅ Section 3

Rohan ate a huge dinner _____ he went to bed.

☐ before

☐ until

☐ for

☐ although

b Which type of conjunction is it? Write your answer below.

2 marks

---

25 Underline the correct spelling in brackets to complete the sentence below. ⬅ Section 8

It was a lovely gift to (receive / receive).

1 mark

26 Circle the correct homophone in brackets to complete the sentence below. ⬅ Section 7

In the hotel we had a whole (sweet / suite) of rooms to ourselves.

1 mark

27 Write a sentence using a preposition of place to describe where you keep your shoes. ⬅ Section 7

1 mark

---

28 Which sentence below uses a parenthesis correctly? Tick **one** box. ⬅ Section 1

☐ We need to leave soon – I hadn't realised it was so late if we want to get there on time.

☐ We need to leave soon – I hadn't realised it was so late – if we want to get there on time.

☐ We need to leave soon I hadn't realised it was so late) if we want to get there on time.

☐ We need to leave soon I hadn't realised it was so late, if we want to get there on time.

1 mark

29 Underline the prepositional phrase in the sentence below. ⬅ Section 2

They told stories around the campfire.

1 mark

30 Complete sentence below by adding a parenthesis with the information that Stockport Viaduct is in Greater Manchester. ⬅ Section 1

Stockport Viaduct _____ was the largest viaduct in the world when it was built, and remains the largest brick structure in UK.

1 mark

31 Circle the correct spelling in brackets to complete the sentence below. ⬅ Section 7

Shall I (pour / poor) the tea?

1 mark

32 Punctuate the sentence below using semi-colons. Section 5

1 mark

If you visit the Eden Project in Cornwall you will experience many amazing things: a colourful garden full of wonderful plants rainforest biomes with enormous trees a vast indoor jungle and even a zip wire.

33 Underline the preposition of direction in the sentence below. Section 2

1 mark

The sprinter was hurtling along the track.

34 Rewrite the sentence below using the correct punctuation. Section 4

1 mark

Where have all the birds gone asked Matilda

_____

_____

35 Which word below has an **ough** sound that rhymes with 'throw'? Tick **one** box. Section 8

☐ though

☐ through

1 mark

☐ thought

36 Rewrite the conversation below using the correct layout of direct speech. Section 4

'Bethan is a bit quiet,' said Arshi, 'Do you think she is worried about something?' 'Maybe,' said Ali, 'She's been like that for a few days now. We need to ask her and see if we can help.' 'Okay, I'll ask her,' replied Arshi, 'We walk home together after school so that's a good time to find out.'

_____

_____

_____

_____

1 mark

_____

37 Is the statement below true or false? Tick **one** box. Section 3

The word 'and' is a coordinating conjunction.

☐ true

1 mark

☐ false

38 In which section is the punctuation mistake? Circle the correct number. Section 4

1 mark

Dinner will be / served at seven o'clock,' / announced the chef / to the hungry crowd.
　　　1　　　　　　　　2　　　　　　　　3　　　　　　　　4

39 Rewrite the sentence below using a contraction. Section 6

1 mark

We shall leave for France in the morning.

_____

_____

40 Underline the parenthesis in the sentence below. `⟵ Section 1` `1 mark`

> Frederico, who comes from Rome, is staying here for two weeks.

41 In which section is the punctuation mistake? Circle the correct number. `⟵ Section 6` `1 mark`

> We've moved all the / table and chairs into / the sports hall because theyr'e / painting the classrooms.
> 1   2   3   4

42 Write two sentences using the homophones below. `⟵ Section 7` `2 marks`

> tide   tied

1 _____

2 _____

43 Which is the correct spelling of the underlined words? Tick **one** box. `⟵ Section 8` `1 mark`

☐ I can't <u>percieve</u> why she would do such a thing.

☐ I can't <u>perceive</u> why she would do such a thing.

44 Which preposition completes the sentence below? Tick **one** box. `⟵ Section 2` `1 mark`

> The River Thames flows _____ Tower Bridge.

☐ throughout

☐ beneath

☐ during

☐ when

45 In which section is the spelling mistake? Circle the correct number. `⟵ Section 9` `1 mark`

> An aplication has / been submitted to the / government for more / funding for the school.
> 1   2   3   4

Time to reflect

Mark your *Progress test* out of 55. How did you do?

Check your answers in the back of the book and write your score in the progress chart.

☐ *0–44 marks*
Use the section links to identify your strengths and weaknesses. Revisit the practice sections you scored the lowest in and then scan the QR code to try more mixed questions.

☐ *45–55 marks*
Use the section links to identify your strengths and weaknesses. You might want to revisit the practice sections you scored the lowest in.

Answers

Diagnostic test

Pages 2–9

1 instructional text

> This is an instructional text because it gives the reader advice on what to do if their pet goes missing.

2 bullet points

3 territorial

4 established themselves

5 It gives the reader hope.

> Try to imagine how this ending would make you feel if you were an owner whose pet was lost.

6 because it is direct speech

> Direct speech is always contained in speech marks.

7 nimble

8 **a** metaphor

> It is a metaphor because the woman's words are compared to a falling pattern without using 'like' or 'as'.

   b Example: The nimble woman's words sound like rain to her because she isn't listening properly.

> Any reasonable answer with an explanation would be correct.

9 **a** no

   b ceased even to pretend to listen

10 Example: Yes, because it is rude not to listen when someone is talking to you.

> Make sure you explain your opinion.

11 **a** Miriam feels afraid.

   b Fear bore down on her like molten lava.

12 transformed into stone

> 'Think about the meaning of the word in context. 'Petrified' can also mean 'afraid', but here it means 'transformed into stone'.

13 barren

14 Example: It suggests that the mountains that have very sharp, dangerous-looking peaks.

> Think about the qualities of a razor.

15 hummed

> 'Chink' would also be correct.

16 **a** old beggars carrying heavy sacks

   b simile

17 The soldiers were so tired they felt drunk.

18 The soldiers' feet were covered in blood.

19 **a** 'Knock-kneed'

> 'Men marched' would also be correct.

   b It shows that they are walking in clumsy way.

> If you chose 'men marched' for question 4a, your answer could be that the alliteration echoes the shuffling of their feet.

20 Example: I don't think that the poet believes this is true because the soldiers' experience sounds horrible, not 'sweet'.

21 Thunder storms, although often very beautiful to watch, can cause huge damage.

> 'Although often very beautiful to watch' can be removed from the sentence without affecting the sense, so it is a parenthesis.

22 John F. Kennedy said: 'Those who dare to fail miserably can achieve greatly.'

23 The ladies' changing room is on the left.

> When a plural ends in an **s** you do not need to add another **s** after the apostrophe.

82

24 brief

25 An alligator's bite will almost always prove fatal.

'An alligator' is singular, so you need an apostrophe and an **s** to show possession.

26 medal

'Meddle' is a verb meaning 'to interfere'.

27 Example: I do my homework after my dinner.

28 throughout the performance

29 Example: I love tennis but I hate football.

Any sentence accurately using 'and', 'but', 'because', 'since' or 'or' would be correct.

30 a towards

   b direction

31 true

Parenthesis is extra information, so it can be removed without affecting the meaning of a sentence.

32 peel

33 To stay safe online you should never do these things: communicate with anyone you do not know; send photos, personal information or details about where you live; send messages to anyone without your parents' or guardians' permission; or arrange to meet anyone you have met online.

A colon is used to introduce the list and semi-colons are used to separate the items because some of them contain commas.

34 The community centre, which is where the pottery classes take place, also has an art gallery.

35 Example: You will need to take: a pencil case, a packed lunch and your PE kit.

36 on

37 a but

   b coordinating

38 'Blue is my favourite colour,' said Arthur.

Direct speech always needs opening and closing speech marks and a closing comma, full stop, question mark or exclamation mark.

39 Dad always takes us to the funfair **whenever** we visit the seaside.

40 The ancient oak tree lay on the ground, its trunk split in half.

41 cough

42 'How long have you been collecting autographs?' asked Ethan. // 'For three years now,' Kwame replied, 'I have thirty three famous people's signatures.' // 'Wow! That's a lot!' exclaimed Ethan, who was clearly impressed, 'Who is the most famous person you have an autograph from?'

You should start a new paragraph each time the speaker changes.

43 true

44 ③

45 I haven't seen that film yet.

46 who is a dental assistant

47 It is the British people's right to vote for the Prime Minister of their choice.

For irregular plurals that don't end in **s**, you add an apostrophe and **s** to show possession.

48 ②

49 true

1 Parenthesis

Page 11

Guided questions

1 We were feeling – as you can imagine – quite nervous by this time.

2 (a famous American President)

3 Finlay – running around hopelessly as usual – couldn't find his PE kit.

4 Bottlenose dolphins **(which live in warm seas all over the world)** eat fish and squid.

5 The headteacher of River View High, who used to teach at my old school, lives quite near to us.

6 Example: Tasha (my big sister) loves football.

> The parenthesis is punctuated with dashes.

> The parenthesis is punctuated with brackets.

> The main clause in this sentence is 'Finlay couldn't find his PE kit'. It still makes sense without the parenthesis.

> The guided answer opens the parenthesis with a bracket, so you must close it with a bracket too.

> The subordinate clause 'who used to teach at my old school' is the parenthesis.

> 'My big sister (Tasha) loves football.' would also be correct.

Page 12

Have a go

1 The Yangtze River, which is 6380 km long, is the third longest river in the world.

2 (the art of growing plants)

3 My eldest brother, who is five years older than me, goes to secondary school.

4 London – my home town – has a population of 8.788 million people.

5 ②

6 Example: The blue whale, which can weigh up to 200 tons, is the largest creature on earth.

> If you take the subordinate clause out, the sentence still makes sense.

> The subordinate clause 'who is five years older than me' is the parenthesis and is punctuated with commas.

> The question doesn't tell you which punctuation to use, so you could use commas, brackets or dashes to punctuate the parenthesis.

> There is a bracket missing at the start of the parenthesis.

> 'The blue whale, which is the largest creature on earth, weighs up to 210 tons.' would also be correct.

Page 13

Timed practice

1 Lerwick, which is the only town in the Shetland Isles, has a population of 7000 people.

2 – which was just before Christmas –

3 Elephants, which are the largest mammals on land, suffer because poachers hunt them for their ivory tusks.

4 Unfortunately, our nearest theme park – **called Wonder World** – is closed for the winter months.

5 Example: When we won the trophy, our coach – who was delighted – bought us all biscuits.

6 ③

7 Example: Beijing (which is the capital of China) has both modern architecture and historic sites.

> The fact that Lerwick is the only town in the Shetland Isles is additional information, so it must be the parenthesis.

> The dashes show where the parenthesis begins and ends.

> The most important information here is that elephants are hunted for their tusks. The additional information about their size is the parenthesis.

> The comma that closes the parenthesis 'dancing with dust particles' is missing.

> 'Beijing (which has both modern architecture and historic states) is the capital of China.' would also be correct.

2 Prepositions

Page 14

Beyond the exam

- Don't risk losing what you already have by trying to get something you think might be better.
- Similar people can often be found together.
- You've misunderstood something or got the wrong idea entirely.

Page 15

Guided questions

1 towards

2 on

3 The biscuits are in the highest cupboard **above** the kettle.

4 Example: I keep my clothes in the wardrobe.

5 It's no use crying **over** spilt milk.

6 School was cancelled today **because of** the snow.

7 a ago
  b time

The word 'highest' suggests that you should use 'above' instead of 'below'.

In this answer 'in' is the preposition, but you could use any appropriate preposition of place.

The preposition 'ago' is used with the simple past tense to show how the past relates to the present.

Page 16

Have a go

1 along

2 a towards
  b direction

3 Nobody has lived in that house **since** Christmas.

4 Example: The bicycle sped along the path.

5 out of

6 true

The preposition 'since' is used with the present perfect tense to show how much time has passed.

Any sentence using an appropriate preposition of direction would be correct.

The preposition 'on' can be used to express time ('on Tuesday') or place ('on the desk').

Page 17

Timed practice

1 by

2 a under
  b place

3 The clock struck loudly **at** midnight.

4 Example: We have art on Tuesday afternoon.

5 on

6 false

Always use 'at' with specific times and 'on' for days ('on Saturday').

Any sentence using an appropriate preposition of time would be correct.

The word 'through' is a preposition of direction.

3 Conjunctions

Page 19

Guided questions

1 a and
  b coordinating

The conjunction 'and' joins the two main clauses together.

Both parts makes sense on their own, so it is a coordinating conjunction.

2 a until

   b subordinating

3 Ashish and Meera were very tired **so** they went to bed early.

4 That is the reason why he wants to leave.

> 'Why' is a subordinating conjunction.

5 false

> Subordinating conjunctions link a main clause and a subordinate clause.

Page 20

Have a go

1 a because

   b subordinating

> 'Because' is a subordinating conjunction. It describes why something happens.

2 nor

> 'Nor' links two main clauses together in the sentence.

3 Example: We went camping again last summer, although it always rains.

> Any sentence using an appropriate subordinating conjunction would be correct.

4 a after

   b subordinating

5 Britain declared war on Germany in 1939 because Hitler invaded Poland.

> The subordinating conjunction is 'because'.

6 true

Page 21

Timed practice

1 a although

   b subordinating

> 'Although' is a subordinating conjunction because it links the main clause with a subordinate clause.

2 a once

   b subordinating

> The conjunction 'once' describes when something will happen, and is therefore subordinating.

3 Grandma would really like to go on a cruise to the Mediterranean **but** she suffers from seasickness.

> The question asks for a coordinating conjunction, so 'yet' would also be correct.

4 Jan is staying at the farmhouse until 15 August.

> The word 'until' is a subordinating conjunction because it describes when something happens.

5 true

6 Example: I always sleep soundly after playing football.

> Any sentence using an appropriate conjunction would be correct.

4 Direct speech

Page 22

Beyond the exam

Example: whispered, sighed, mumbled

Example: screamed, shouted, exclaimed

Page 23

Guided questions

1 'My tablet has stopped working!' exclaimed Ali.

> - In the first option, the exclamation mark is missing at the end of the speech.
> - In the second option, the exclamation mark is outside the closing speech mark.
> - In the fourth option, the opening speech mark is missing.

2 'Dragons are legendary creatures that feature in many stories,' replied Nathan.

> You must include all necessary punctuation.

3 ③

> The opening speech mark is missing before 'quick'.

4 'Where is everyone?' yelled Martha looking around the playground. **//** 'I'm not sure,' replied Yasmin, 'I think they're all still in class.' **//** 'But it's 10.30. They should be out by now,' said Martha looking around in disappointment. **//** 'I think they have to stay in and finish their project,' replied Yasmin.

5 '<u>what</u> time does the cricket match start?' asked Michael, 'we don't want to be late.'

'<u>probably</u> at one o'clock' answered Wayne, 'at least that's what Ivy said.'

6 Example: 'Are you hungry yet, Conor?' asked Mum.

'Yes! I'm always starving after swimming!' replied Connor.

'It must be all that hard work,' smiled Mum, 'how does pizza sound?'

Page 24

Have a go

1 Huan tiptoed up and whispered, 'Shh … the deer are behind the bush.'

- The first option is correct.
- In the second option, the full stop is outside of the closing speech mark.
- In the third option, the closing speech mark is missing.

2 After the match Ted yelled, 'Yes, we won again!'

An exclamation mark is correct because Ted is yelling.

3 Example: 'We did long division all afternoon. It was so boring!' sighed Masa.

'Well at least you weren't outside doing PE in the rain,' replied Simon, 'I'd much rather be doing maths in a nice, warm classroom.'

Masa giggled and said, 'Maybe we should swap places!'

4 ③

The exclamation mark is missing from the end of the speech.

5 'I can't wait to go to the theme park next weekend,' exclaimed Bridgette. **//** 'I'm looking forward to it too,' cried Sally,' Which rides do you most want to go on?' **//** 'Not sure, I definitely want to do the Red River Rapids, what about you?' **//** 'The Space Race is my favourite.'

6 '<u>this</u> carrot cake is delicious,' said Katie, 'did you bake it yourself?'

'<u>not</u> completely' admitted Aika, 'my dad helped me.'

Page 25

Timed practice

1 'The rain is coming!' shouted the tour guide. 'Get inside quickly!'

- The first option is correct.
- In the second option, the opening speech mark is missing.
- In third option, the exclamation mark is outside the closing speech mark.
- In the fourth option, the opening speech mark is missing from the second part of speech.

2 'Where have you been?' demanded the teacher when we arrived ten minutes late.

3 ④

The closing speech mark is missing after 'him!'

4 'What are you going to do with all those blackberries,' asked Tim. **//** 'I'm going to makes pies and jams,' replied Aunt Nancy, 'They will be delicious with cream.' **//** 'Mmm,' replied Tim licking his lips, 'Can mum and I come round to your house for supper soon?'

5 '<u>we</u> are going to plant a vegetable patch in the garden next Spring,' said Julien. '<u>in</u> the corner by the greenhouse.'

'<u>will</u> you grow carrots?' asked Sheena.

6 Example: 'Do you like rock music?' asked Emma.

'It's okay,' replied Tisha, 'But I prefer country music.'

'But country music is so boring!' teased Emma.

5 Colons, semi-colons and dashes

Guided questions

1 The famous inventor Thomas Edison once said: 'I've not failed. I've just found 10 000 ways that won't work.'

> The colon is placed directly before the quotation it introduces.

2 When making meringues you should always whip the egg whites until they are stiff: if you don't the mixture won't rise.

> The second clause provides an explanation of the first – it tells you more about why you whip the egg whites.

3 Dromedary camels have one hump; Bactrian camels have two humps.

4 I love reading science fiction stories: they really make me think.

> The second clause provides more information about why the writer likes science fiction stories, so a colon is correct.

5 Example: On Mum's birthday we will: make pancakes for breakfast, go for a walk and visit Grandad.

> The list is introduced by a colon, so using semi-colons instead of commas would also be correct.

6 You will have a great choice of activities at the camp: windsurfing; hiking up magnificent, heather-covered hillsides; canoeing around the huge, blue lake; and swimming.

> Some of the items in the list contain commas, so they must be separated by semi-colons.

7 true

Have a go

1 Many crops are grown on the farm: butternut squash to name one.

2 Vivien Greene famously said: 'Life isn't about waiting for the storm to pass, it's about dancing in the rain.'

> The opening speech mark shows you where the quotation starts.

3 Most tea is produced in China; most coffee comes from Brazil.

4 I dislike everything about that café: the cold, burnt toasties; the horrible, uncomfortable chairs; the bad music and the rude owner.

5 Example: For the party we will need: glasses, fizzy drinks, music and a cake.

> The items in this list are all single words, so they can be separated by commas.

6 I have so much homework to do this weekend: a long, tedious history essay; two pages of difficult French exercises; and some geography.

Timed practice

1 She's not coming to the party: she's got the flu.

2 The days are very short in winter; they are very long in summer.

3 The friends were totally exhausted: they had walked 15 miles.

> The second clause provides an explanation of the first. The friends were exhausted because they had walked 15 miles.

4 Dad's special salad recipe includes: fresh, free-range eggs**;** delicious, salty olives**;** crisp lettuce**;** and ripe cherry tomatoes.

> If you use semi-colons to punctuate a list, remember to include one before the final item.

5 I can't believe he said that – it was so funny!

> A dash is more appropriate than a colon here because the sentence is informal.

6 Example: We will need to pack: sun cream, water, a tent and sunglasses.

> If the items in your list contain commas, you would need to punctuate them with semi-colons.

7 false

6 Apostrophes

Page 31

Guided questions

1 **We'll** be able to find out **who's** coming from the guest list.

> Both 'we shall' and 'we will' become 'we'll' when contracted.

2 The ladies' changing room is on the far side of the sports centre.

> The plural noun is 'ladies' so the apostrophe goes after the **s**.

3 My mum's car is really old.

> 'My mum' is singular, so the apostrophe goes before the **s**.

4 The cooker's handle has fallen off.

5 ③

> 'Mandys team' should be 'Mandy's team'.

6 Example: The students' books are on the desks.

> Remember, for regular plurals ending in **s** you only add an apostrophe.

7 false

> 'Its' shows possession but does not have an apostrophe, like 'his' and 'hers'. 'It's' is a contraction of 'it is'.

Page 32

Have a go

1 **Don't** take drinks into the classroom.

2 He'll need to get more paint to finish the painting.

3 The women's business is a great success.

> 'Women' is an irregular plural, so you need to add an apostrophe and **s**.

4 girls'

> More than one girl will be running in the race, so 'girls' is a regular plural and does not need an extra **s**.

5 Joshua's book is in his bag.

> Joshua owns the book so you need to add an apostrophe and **s**.

6 ④

> 'it's' should be 'its'.

7 **She'd** love it there – the scenery is beautiful.

Page 33

Timed practice

1 I **haven't** been to Blackpool for ages.

2 The torches' beams shone on their startled faces.

> Treat plurals ending in **es** as regular plurals. Add an apostrophe but no extra **s**.

3 The dancers' costumes looked fantastic.

4 should've

5 The farmer's tractor is extremely muddy.

6 ①

> 'Plants leaves' should be 'plants' leaves'.

7 Sunil paid a lot for his phone; he **could've** saved money if **he'd** shopped around.

8 Example: Our neighbours' dog is really friendly.

> Any sentence that accurately uses a possessive apostrophe would be correct.

Checkpoint 1

Pages 34–35

1 If our team wins the match on Saturday (and everyone thinks they will) we will go and watch the final next month.

> The parenthesis is 'and everyone thinks they will'. It would also be correct to use dashes.

2 The firemen's helmets are designed to protect them from heat and falling cinders

> 'Firemen' is plural.

3 'My favourite films are action movies,' said Joshua.

4 between

5 To avoid catching colds and spreading germs you should always: wash your hands before eating, put used tissues in the bin and never share cups with other people.

6 ②

> The parenthesis is 'semiaquatic mammals' so the second bracket should come after 'mammals' and before 'are'.

7 'The cruise ship has now docked in the port,' announced Mr Wilson.

8

	coordinating	subordinating
because		✓
while		✓
nor	✓	
but	✓	

9 true

> Only add an apostrophe to 'its' when you want to say 'it is'.

7 Homophones and homonyms

Page 37

Guided questions

1 a patients
   b prophet
   c advice

> 'Patience' means 'the ability to stay calm and not become annoyed'.

> 'Profit' means 'financial gain' or 'advantage'.

2 Example: The school trip costs ten pounds.

3 whose

> 'Who's' is incorrect because its expanded form ('who is') does not fit in the sentence.

4 a I am auditioning for a **main** part in the play.
   b The huge lion has an enormous, scraggy **main**.

5 Examples: My dog always barks at cats in the street.
   This oak tree has a very thick bark.

> Any two sentences that show the two meanings of 'bark' would be correct.

Page 38

Have a go

1 a lone
   b allowed
   c devise

> In **ise/ice** pairs like this, the word ending in **ise** is usually a verb and the word ending in **ice** is usually a noun.

2 Example: 'Rose' is the past tense of the verb 'rise'.

3 descent

4 a The boy stands and **stares** at the beautiful view.

   b Go up the **stairs** to the x-ray clinic.

5 Examples: He stands by his principles.

   Mrs Roberts is the principal of the academy.

> Any two sentences that show both meanings of the homophone would be correct.

6 false

Page 39

Timed practice

1 a <u>cereal</u>

> 'Serial' means 'broken into parts', or 'part of a series'.

   b <u>heir</u>

> 'Heir' has a silent 'h, so it sounds the same as 'air'.

   c <u>licence</u>

> 'License' is a verb meaning 'to give permission'.

2 Example: An 'address' is the place where someone lives.

3 <u>they're</u>

> 'They're' is a contraction of 'they are'. 'There' indicates place.

4 a I'll phone you in the **morning**.

   b Howard's great grandfather died yesterday so his whole family is in **mourning**.

> Homophones sound the same but are spelled differently.

5 Examples: The sky is a beautiful blue today.

   The wind blew all the leaves off the trees.

6 true

8 ie/ei and ough spellings

Page 41

Guided questions

1 a (achievement)
   b (conceived)

> Both of these words make an /ee/ sound, so they follow the 'i before e except after c' rule.

2 fields

3 mantelpiece

4 sought

5 dough

> The **ough** sound in 'dough' rhymes with 'show'.

6 ③

> 'Cogh' should be spelled 'cough'.

7 Example: Yesterday I received a letter from my aunt in the post.

> The /ee/ sound in 'received' is spelled **ei** because it has a **c** immediately before it.

8 fought

Page 42

Have a go

1 a (conceited)
   b (niece)

> The /ee/ sound in 'niece' is spelled **ie** because it does not have a **c** immediately before it.

2 mischief

3 brief

4 babies

5 enough

> The **ough** sound in 'plough' rhymes with 'now'.

6 plough

> 'Boght' should be spelled 'bought'.

7 ①

> The 'i before e' rule only works with the /ee/ sound.

8 false

Timed practice

1 a (perceive)

  b (relief)

2 calor**ies** •————————————— 'Calories' has a **c** in it, but it doesn't affect the **ie** because it is not right next to it.

3 thi**ef**

4 though

5 ② •————————————————————— 'Thourt' should be spelled 'thought'.

6 I had a **piece** of chocolate cake for dessert.

7 true •————————————————————— For example, 'nought', 'thought' or 'brought'.

8 a Example: On Saturday I bought a new computer game and some magazines.

  b Example: snort

9 Tricky spellings

Page 45

Guided questions

1 secret

2 The new series is **marvellous**. •————— **Vel** is the stressed syllable in 'marvel', so the **l** is doubled when you add a suffix.

3 ④ •————————————————————— 'Medcine' should be spelled 'medicine'.

4 gu**a**rantee

5 I referred to an atlas to help with my homework.

6 **Sadly**, my best friend couldn't come on the school trip. •————— The suffix **ly** begins with a consonant, so you don't need to double the **d** at the end of the root word.

7 ④

Page 46

Have a go

1 a frightening

  b restaurant

2 Rajesh is always the winner when we play board games. •————— 'Win' follows the consonant-vowel-consonant pattern, so you double the final letter before you add the suffix.

3 ④ •————————————————————— 'Languige' should be spelled 'language'.

4 cutting

5 enviro**n**ment •————————————————————— **N** is a silent letter in 'environment'.

6 My sister **answered** the phone.

7 My little brother's favourite puzzle is spot the **difference**.

8 Example: They cheered and danced around madly.

Page 47

Timed practice

1 secretary •————————————————————— The **a** in 'secretary' is silent or makes an /ee/ sound depending on how you pronounce it.

2 corresponding

3 a 'Ouch,' cried Dad, rub**bing** his toe.

b We've been plan**ning** the trip for ages.

4 After he was caught cheating, he was omitted from the competition.

Mit is the stressed syllable in the root word 'omit', so you must double the last letter before adding the suffix.

5 ①

'Recommendded' should be spelled 'recommended', because **mend** is the stressed syllable in the root word 'recommend'.

6 vegetables

7 bad**ly**

Fin is the stressed syllable in the root word 'finish', so you do not need to double the **h** when you add the suffix.

8 Can I have dessert now I've **finished** my dinner?

9 guitar

Checkpoint 2

Pages 48–49

1 mist

'Mist' is a noun and is like fog. 'Missed' is a verb.

2 diesel

3 I think it would be interesting to go and live abroad in a foreign country.

4 ③

The correct spelling is 'hindrance'.

5 necessary

6 Example: My favourite season is Spring.
I was so happy I had a spring in my step!

7 true

8 environment

There is a silent 'n' in environment.

9 stationery

'Stationery' means writing equipment. 'Stationary' means not moving.

10 tough

11 competition

12 piece

10 Understanding texts

Page 51

Guided questions

1 informal newspaper report

First-person accounts in newspaper reports often use an informal style.

2 because it is direct speech

3 a false

b points are awarded for authenticity and volume

The text doesn't directly state this. You have to infer it from what the text tells you points are awarded for.

4 a because they want the public to learn more about deer

b The championships provide a fun way for people to come along and learn about the red deer and their environment.

5 ultimate

Make sure you think about the meaning of words in context. 'Ultimate' can mean 'final' or 'last', but here it means 'best'.

Have a go

1 present tense

2 amplify

3 a to make the atmosphere seem tense

   b very loud

4 expectant

> 'Expectant' is the adjective form of the verb 'to expect'.

Page 53

Timed practice

1 'Remote' means far away from towns and cities.

> Any answer that explains this meaning would be correct.

2 passive voice

> The passive voice is often used in formal texts such as reports.

3 subheading

4 pricket

5 a true

   b herbivores

> Herbivores only eat vegetation. Carnivores only eat meat. Omnivores eat both.

6 helpless

11 Explaining texts

Page 55

Guided questions

1 a first person

   b to help the reader understand Christabel's point of view

> The first person uses 'I' ('I am'). The third person uses 'he' or 'she' ('she is').

2 because it is direct speech

> Words recorded exactly as the person said them are placed inside inverted commas (speech marks).

3 a false

   b late

> The word 'late' in this context means someone who is no longer alive.

4 has modern, well-informed decisions

5 It is effective because it moves the focus from Christabel to the duty that all women have.

> Although the text wasn't written by Christobel Pankhurst, the writer has chosen to present it in the form of her imagined diary to make it more personal and bring the historical time to life.

Page 56

Have a go

1 a false

   b occasionally aggressive measures

> 'Aggressive' means 'forceful' or 'confrontational'.

2 emancipation

> 'Emancipation' means being set free from legal restrictions.

3 It inspires the reader to stand up for their beliefs.

4 era

5 Because giving an example helps the reader understand what types of measures the suffragettes took.

Page 57

Timed practice

1 a letter

   b It helps to bring the past to life for the reader.

> The greeting ('Dear Olivia') and sign off ('Your loving friend, Christabel') show that it is a letter.

2 imprisonment

3 elect

4 Your sacrifice won't have been in vain. •————————————

5 to leave Olivia with a positive and motivational message

> If you don't know a word you can often work out its meaning from the rest of the sentence.

12 Giving your opinion

Page 59

Guided questions

1 because she couldn't find the porter •————————————

> The text says: 'The porter was nowhere of course.'

2 Example: It is effective because it shows that she hated being back there so much that it was painful to her.

3 sordid

4 The woman is quite wealthy and looks out of place in the sooty railway station. •————————————

> The writer contrasts the woman's wealthy appearance with the shabby surroundings of the station.

5 she said in her bright voice. But she was not feeling bright.

6 Example: I feel sorry for Harry because the woman doesn't really like him. •————————————

> Always back up your opinion with a reason.

Page 60

Have a go

1 onomatopoeia •————————————

> Onomatopoeia is when words sound like the noise they describe.

2 **a** personification •————————————
    b She was confident.

> The goal is personified as a foolish person.

3 Parveen feels as though she is moving in slow motion.

4 Example: Yes, because she should not let the bullies stop her from doing her best. •————————————

> Any opinion is acceptable, as long as you explain it clearly.

Page 61

Timed practice

1 Jacob raced into the cloakroom

2 **a** leading his brave troops into battle
    b It shows that he thinks the fight will be dramatic and exciting, like a battle. •————————————

> Metaphors compare things without using 'like' or 'as'.

3 He is generous.

4 Example: I think Jacob is very kind because he gives his boots to his brother even though it means he can't join in the snowball fight. •————————————

> Remember to explain why this is your opinion of Jacob.

13 Explaining poetry

Page 63

Guided questions

1 **a** the laughter of the logs
    b personification •————————————

> It is personification because the logs are given the human quality of laughter.

2 a More fair than roses

   b simile

> 'The flowers of the fire' and 'metaphor' would also be correct.

3 a snipes are silent

   b alliteration

4 It creates a contrast between the first part and the second part.

> The words in the first part describe cold and stillness, whereas the words in the second part describe warmth and life. This creates a contrast between the two sections.

5 Example: This poem makes me feel happy about winter because it talks about snowy hillsides and log fires.

> Any clearly explained opinion would be correct.

Page 64

Have a go

1 The eagle is surrounded by sky.

> The eagle is up on a cliff or 'crag', so the blue around him must be sky.

2 a And like a thunderbolt he falls.

   b simile

3 a personification

   b Example: The sea sounds very small and unimportant in contrast to the eagle because it only 'crawls'.

> Crawling is associated with babies, so the personification gives the sea similar qualities of weakness.

4 He feels a sense of awe and admiration.

Page 65

Timed practice

1 a hope

   b metaphor

> The whole poem presents the bird as a metaphor for hope.

2 a alliteration

   b to recreate the sound of the sea

> The repetition of 's' in 'strangest sea' could sound like the waves crashing below.

3 Hope has given comfort to many people in difficult times.

4 Example: I think that the writer has lost hope in the past because she is able to describe how it feels to be scared and lonely and what it is like when hope returns.

> Make sure you explain your opinion in detail.

Checkpoint 3

Pages 66–69

1 a personification

   b Tossing their heads in sprightly dance.

> Here, the daffodils are given the human quality of dancing.

2 He feels sad.

3 simile

> It is a simile because the daffodils are compared to the stars using 'as'.

4 margins

5 Example: I think the writer feels excited because he sees thousands of daffodils that are beautiful and look like they are dancing.

> Always back up your opinion with a reason.

6 a They have hairs in the centre of the palms.

   b It makes the Count's hands seem like an animal's paws.

> The key word 'hands' shows you where in the text to look for this information.

7 a Example: He feels disgusted and sick.

   b He is secretly pleased by the narrator's reaction.

8 protuberant

> Even if you don't know the meaning of this word, you can guess it from the context of the sentence.

9 a music

  b Example: It shows that the Count likes the horrible howling noise, which makes him seem even more scary.

Any opinion would be correct, as long as you explain it.

10 metaphor

Metaphors compare things without using 'like' or 'as'.

11 a his acts being seven ages

  b Example: I think this is a good comparison because it suggests that life is a story with lots of different scenes, just like a play.

12 Everybody is born and dies.

13 Example: I don't think the writer likes babies because he describes them using the negative words 'mewling' and 'puking'.

14 whining

15 a simile

  b He walks very slowly because he doesn't want to go to school.

It is a simile because it compares the boy to a snail using 'like'.

16 to persuade people to buy a brand of trainers

17 to make sure that the reader remembers the name of the shoes

18 durable

19 alliteration

20 investing

21 to persuade readers to buy the shoes quickly

22 Example: I don't think it is right for people to spend so much on one pair of trainers when they could buy a cheaper pair and then give the extra money to charity.

14 Writing Non-Fiction

Page 70

Guided question

1 a Mind map completed with suitable ideas answering prompt questions.

  b Reflect on how I feel about it now. **conclusion**

  Describe what happened and how it felt. **middle**

  Set the scene and explain who was there. **introduction**

This is a sensible structure to use in any question that asks you to describe an event.

Page 71

Guided question

1 Example: My favourite hobby is rugby. I **enjoy** it because **it keeps me fit and gives me the opportunity to spend time with my friends outdoors**.

When I first started playing I was **not very confident**. For example, I **wouldn't run to catch the ball or tackle other players**. Luckily my coach is really supportive and helped me improve. Now I **am one of the most active players on the field and often win 'Man of the Match'**.

Any answer that makes sense and uses a suitable level of formality is acceptable.

Page 72

Guided question

1 Answers should include interesting language choices and maintain a suitable level of formality.

Have a go

1 Answers should include interesting language choices and maintain a suitable level of formality. They should be structured with a clear introduction, middle and conclusion and use correct punctuation and grammar throughout.

Page 73

Timed practice

Use the checklist on page 73 to assess how successful your writing is. Tick each feature you have achieved, and note the others as targets for future writing.

> Use the checklist on page 73 to assess how successful your writing is. Tick each feature you have achieved, and note the others as targets for future writing.

> You could also ask a friend or family member to read your writing and answer these questions:
> - Did you enjoy the story?
> - Did the structure make sense?
> - Was the language appropriate?
> - Was the spelling and punctuation correct?

Progress test

Pages 74–81

1 biodiversity

2 rain, snow, sleet or hail

3 true

4 the resources that we get from the rainforest

5 the world's largest pharmacy

> You can use the key word 'medicine' to help you find which part of the text to look in for this phrase.

6 Any two of: medicines, rubber, chocolate, bamboo, nuts, vanilla.

7 a Example: They allow it because it creates jobs and money.
  b Example: I believe that they shouldn't be allowed to do this because the rainforest is home to many special animals that can't live anywhere else.

> You can give any opinion as long as you explain it.

8 the harbour

9 a The light from the lantern is very weak.
  b personification

> The lantern is given the human quality of being shy.

10 squat

> You can infer the meaning from the context of 'little' and 'railway engine'.

11 carved out of solid darkness

12 The bags were wrapped up in sausage shapes.

13 a simile
  b Example: It makes the town sound very pretty, like a decorated box.

> It is a simile because the houses are compared to shells using 'like'.

14 a She imagines it swimming towards the boat.
  b personification

> The landing stage is given the human action of swimming.

15 Example: I think that Grandma is a kind and caring person because of the way she speaks to her son. I also think she is worried about the journey because the text says she is 'very agitated'.

> Make sure you give a reason for your opinion.

16 'When will we meet our new neighbours?' asked Shelly.

17 ③ — The opening speech mark before 'fortunately' is missing.

18 Example: Our school (**called Moorside Junior**) has six classes in each year group.

19 Grandpa's tools are locked in the shed.

20 a but
   b coordinating — 'But' links two main clauses, so it is a coordinating conjunction.

21 The women's toilets are on the right. — When showing possession, add an apostrophe and **s** to irregular plurals that don't end in **s**.

22 The former American President Theodore Roosevelt said**:** 'It's hard to fail, but it is worse never to have tried to succeed.' — Use a colon to introduce a quotation or list.

23 parliament

24 a before — 'Before' links a main clause and a subordinate clause, so it is a subordinating conjunction.
   b subordinating

25 receive

26 (suite) — A 'suite' is a set of rooms. 'Sweet' is an adjective describing a pleasant taste.

27 Example: I keep my shoes under my bed.

28 We need to leave soon – I hadn't realised it was so late – if we want to get there on time. — You could also punctuate this example with a pair of brackets.

29 around the campfire

30 Example: Stockport Viaduct (**in Greater Manchester**) was the largest viaduct in the world when it was built, and remains the largest brick structure in UK.

31 (pour) — 'Pour' is a verb meaning 'to tip out a liquid'. Poor is an adjective meaning 'lacking in money' or 'bad quality'.

32 If you visit the Eden Project in Cornwall you will experience these amazing things**:** a colourful garden full of wonderful plants**;** rainforest biomes with enormous trees**;** a vast indoor jungle**;** and even a zip wire. — If you punctuate a list with semi-colons, make sure you add a semi-colon before the final item.

33 along

34 'Where have all the birds gone**?**' asked Matilda**.**

35 though

36 'Bethan is a bit quiet,' said Arshi, 'Do you think she's worried about something?' — Start a new paragraph each time the speaker changes.

   'Maybe,' said Ali, 'She's been like that for a few days now. We need to ask her and see if we can help.'

   'Okay I'll ask her,' replied Arshi, 'We walk home together after school so that's a good time to find out.'

37 true — 'And' links two main clauses, so it is a coordinating conjunction.

38 ① — The opening speech mark is missing.

39 We'll leave for France in the morning.

40 <u>who comes from Rome</u>

41 ③ •————————————————————————————————————— 'They're' is a contraction of 'they are', so the apostrophe should be after the **y** to show the missing **a**.

42 Examples: It will be high tide at five o'clock. •——— Any two sentences that show the meanings
    The boat is tied to the jetty.   of the two words would be correct.

43 perceive

44 The River Thames flows beneath Tower Bridge.

45 ① •————————————————————————————————————— The correct spelling is 'application'.

Progress chart

Use this chart to keep track of your 11+ journey. Fill in your marks as you complete each *Timed practice* section and check off any extra practice you do.

	Timed practice	Digital questions	Ten-minute test
Diagnostic test	☐ /57		
1 Parenthesis	☐ /7	☑	☑
2 Prepositions	☐ /7	☑	☑
3 Conjunctions	☐ /8	☑	☑
4 Direct speech	☐ /7	☑	☑
5 Colons, semi-colons and dashes	☐ /7	☑	☑
6 Apostrophes	☐ /8	☑	☑
Checkpoint 1	☐ /10	☑	
7 Homophones and homonyms	☐ /10	☑	☑
8 ie/ei and ough spellings	☐ /10	☑	☑
9 Tricky spellings	☐ /10	☑	☑
Checkpoint 2	☐ /13	☑	
10 Understanding texts	☐ /7	☑	☑
11 Explaining texts	☐ /6	☑	☑
12 Giving your opinion	☐ /6	☑	☑
13 Explaining poetry	☐ /7	☑	☑
Checkpoint 3	☐ /31	☑	
14 Writing non-fiction			☑
Progress test	☐ /55	☑	

Published by Pearson Education Limited, 80 Strand, London, WC2R 0RL.

www.pearsonschools.co.uk

Text © Pearson Education Limited 2018
Edited, typeset and produced by Elektra Media Ltd
Original illustrations © Pearson Education Limited
Illustrated by Elektra Media Ltd
Cover design by Lukas Bischoff

The right of Helen Thomson to be identified as author of this work has been asserted by her in accordance with the Copyright, Designs and Patents Act 1988.

First published 2018

21 20 19 18
10 9 8 7 6 5 4 3 2 1

British Library Cataloguing in Publication Data
A catalogue record for this book is available from the British Library

ISBN: 978 1 292 24645 1

Printed in Slovakia by Neografia

Acknowledgements
Pearson acknowledges use of the following extract on page 4: Thomson, Helen M, *Stolen Destinies*; first edition; © 2012, CreateSpace Independent Publishing Platform.
We would like to thank Antonia Maxwell and Steph Niland for their invaluable help in the development and trialling of this publication.

Note from the publisher
Pearson has robust editorial processes, including answer and fact checks, to ensure the accuracy of the content in this publication, and every effort is made to ensure this publication is free of errors. We are, however, only human, and occasionally errors do occur. Pearson is not liable for any misunderstandings that arise as a result of errors in this publication, but it is our priority to ensure that the content is accurate. If you spot an error, please do contact us at resourcescorrections@pearson.com so we can make sure it is corrected.